BIRTH OF THE LUFTWAFFE FIGHTER FORCE

The Hall of Mirrors at Versailles. It was here that the Allies sought to suppress the threat of German rearmament following the First World War.

Germany is forbidden to maintain either land or sea forces... Germany is to surrender all her land and water aircraft, including any which may be in the process of manufacture, development, or construction... This order also covers aircraft engines, ballonets, and wings, armaments, ammunition, airborne instruments, wireless equipment, photographic equipment (including film cameras)...

For a period of six months after the present Treaty becomes effective, Germany is forbidden to manufacture or to import aircraft or aircraft parts...

Extracts from Part V, Articles 198, 201 and 202 of the Treaty of Versailles

28 June 1919

LEFT: The Treaty of Versailles called for the surrender and destruction of most of Germany's military aircraft and precluded the existence of an air force. This photo shows a number of partially completed aircraft left outside an assembly shop at the DFW factory in Leipzig-Lindenthal in 1918. These aircraft were subsequently scrapped under the terms of the Treaty.

RIGHT: Hptm. Bruno Loerzer, at this time commander of Jasta 26 poses by his Albatros D Va in 1917. Loerzer was awarded the Pour le Mérite on 18 February 1918 and later took over command of Jagdgeschwader 3. The careers of Loerzer and Göring had been closely allied during the First World War and when the latter became C-in-C of the Luftwaffe, Loerzer commanded one of the first of the new fighter Geschwader, JG 232.

During the First World War, Walther Wever, although only a Hauptmann, had been appointed as Ludendorff's Adjutant. In 1935 this able and far-sighted officer was appointed as the Luftwaffe's first Chief of Air Staff. One of his earliest ideas was to propose the construction of a four-engined strategic bomber which "must be capable of flying right around Britain under combat conditions." Wever was killed on 3 June 1936 when an aircraft which he was piloting crashed and was destroyed.

Hans Jürgen Stumpff, who ultimately held the rank of Generaloberst, was born in 1890, serving with the German Army and appointed to the General Staff in 1916. In 1933 he transferred to the Luftwaffe, becoming head of the Personnel Office. From June 1937 to January 1939 he was Chief of the General Staff and then took over Luftflotte 1 early in 1940.

General Hellmuth Felmy, head of Luftwaffengruppenkommando 2 in February 1938, was commissioned by Stumpff to investigate what war with Britain would mean. Felmy was to conclude that the Luftwaffe could not possibly be ready for a major war in 1939.

Hugo Sperrle, who eventually reached the rank of Generalfeldmarschall, was born in 1885 and served with the Luftstreitkräfte during the First World War. He then remained with the Reichswehr, transferring to the Luftwaffe in 1935. Following a short period in command of the Legion Condor he took over command of Luftwaffengruppenkommando 3.

Breaking the shackles

The signing of the Treaty of Versailles in June 1919 following the end of the First World War, officially signalled the collapse of military aviation in Germany. At the end of the war, Germany possessed some 20,000 military aircraft, of which 2,400 were bomber, fighter and reconnaissance machines. In accordance with the Treaty, 15,000 of these machines were surrendered together with 27,000 aero engines.

However, despite the massive military and political implications of such restrictions, the victorious Allies could not prevent the Germans from at least thinking about the future of air power – whatever it may hold – and from drawing upon the strategic and tactical experiences of the air war they had recently fought.

One man blessed with sufficient precognition about the future was the cunning head of the *Reichswehr, Generaloberst* Hans von Seeckt. One week after taking over the *Truppenamt* – essentially the former German General Staff – von Seeckt wrote: "It is absolutely necessary to put the experience of the war in a broad light and to collect this experience while impressions won on the battlefield are still fresh..."

As early as 1920, von Seeckt, regarded by one historian as "one of the most brilliant, energetic and imaginative of the old school of German General Staff officers", recognised the importance of air power and, more especially, that Germany would, undoubtedly, need an air force at some stage in the future. Undeterred by the shackle of foreign demands – indeed ignoring them – von Seeckt's first move was to select a small group of some 180 officers, many of whom were former pilots from the from the Great War, as the nucleus of a "Central Flying Office", or *Fliegerzentrale,* within the *Reichswehr*. The names of some of the young officers belonging to this group bear testimony to von Seeckt's insight – Felmy, Sperrle, Wever, Kesselring and Stumpff – all to become accomplished senior commanders of the future *Luftwaffe.* Having selected this group, von Seeckt then did all he could to both protect them against the sceptics in both the government and the military and to allow them to promote their ideas regarding the contemporary use of air power. Formed into committees, these officers began to write reports and papers, examining every aspect of air war doctrine.

The head of the post-war Reichswehr (German Armed Forces), Generaloberst Hans von Seeckt who, after his appointment in 1920, immediately collected together a small group of former pilots from the Great War to form the nucleus of a "Fliegerzentrale" (Central Flying Office). This was to lay the foundations for the new Luftwaffe.

Additionally, by March 1920, von Seeckt had established a modest network of aviation departments with organisational and training representatives in the *Truppenamt* – effectively the General Staff; an intelligence officer who was to monitor the development of foreign air forces; an Air Technical Office (*Technisches Amt*) within the Army Ordnance Office or *Heereswaffenamt;* and an Air Armament Economics Office or *Fliegerrüstungwirtschaftliches Referat.*

von Seeckt's dynamism began to pay off, if not in terms of actually creating an air force, then at least in terms of covertly encouraging practical debate on all aspects of military aviation theory. One such committee dealt with fighter tactics. It consisted of three *Pour le Mérite* fighter aces and several wartime tactical air commanders. A number of key issues were debated by the committee including the maximum strength of fighter *Gruppen.* Opinion varied widely between the former ace pilots and their commanders but eventually it was agreed that there should be six *Staffeln* per *Gruppe.* The question of whether the *Gruppe* or the *Geschwader* should serve as the tactical unit arose and this was agreed on the former.

A third question dealt with the deployment of one- and two-seat fighters. Certain officers felt that fighter *Gruppen* should be equipped only with single-seat aircraft, whilst others opted for a mix of both type of machine. There were discussions on the feasibility of placing more than one *Gruppe* of fighters under one tactical commander, with the ace pilots stating that it would be impractical for one officer to command more than one *Gruppe,* though it was recognised that

Albert Kesselring, seen here as a Generalfeldmarschall, was born in 1895 and served with the German Army during the First World War. He transferred to the still-secret Luftwaffe in 1933, serving for a short time as Chief of General Staff. In 1938 he took over command of Luftwaffen-gruppenkommando 1 and later transferred to Luftflotte 2.

BELOW: Oblt. Hermann Göring in the cockpit of his all white Fokker D VII. Better known for his activities before and during the Second World War, Göring scored 22 victories during the earlier conflict and was awarded the Pour le Mérite in 1918.

RIGHT: Hermann Göring poses by his all white Fokker D VII. The serial number of his machine, Fok.D VII F 5125/18, was painted on the lower part of the fuselage, the latter figure indicating its year of manufacture. Göring commanded first Jasta 27 and then JG 1, the first "Jagdgeschwader Richthofen". Some idea of Göring's future politics can be gained from the following incident. At the end of the First World War, JG 1 returned to Darmstadt where Communist soldier-councils took away the weapons of the first section to land. Hearing of this, Göring peremptorily ordered: "Weapons back or I attack with the whole Geschwader!". Needless to say their weapons were returned.

ABOVE: A number of pilots that served with the Luftstreitkräfte during the First World War were to serve with the Luftwaffe during the second. Here Erich Mix (with the stick) stands in front of his Fokker D VII. Mix was later to command III./JG 2 and eventually became Kommodore of JG 1 in August 1942 before becoming a staff officer.

BELOW: At the end of the war many of Germany's military aircraft were destroyed under the Treaty of Versailles. These Albatros J I and J II armoured close support aircraft are shown in the process of being scrapped at the Albatros factory at Schneidemühl near Eisenach.

ABOVE: This Albatros D V fighter was flown by Lt. Paul Billik whilst serving with Jasta 12. By the end of the First World War he had scored a total of 31 victories, was commanding Jasta 52 and had been nominated for the Pour le Mérite. He was killed on 8 March 1926 while testing a Junkers F 13. It is interesting to note that Billik's aircraft carries a Hakenkreuz as a personal emblem. An ancient emblem and one that was thought to bring good luck, the Hakenkreuz was later adopted as the emblem of the Nazi Party in 1922.

ultimately such a decision rested on the progress made in radio development.

Despite constructive – though covert – military redevelopment, the German aircraft manufacturing industry was dealt a blow by the Treaty of Versailles which stated that for a period of six months from the date of effect, Germany was forbidden to manufacture or to import aircraft or aircraft parts. Furthermore, the Paris Agreements of late January 1921, forbade the German government to allow the manufacture of aircraft and associated equipment until three months after the date on which the Inter-Allied Aviation Commission had confirmed Germany's total compliance with the aforementioned Treaty terms.

The results of an Allied conference – the so-called Ambassadors Conference – decreed on 14 April 1922 that further limitations were to be implemented in line with the "definitions" of aircraft as set by this conference. These definitions were specifically intended to disallow the development of military aircraft by imposing performance limits of 177 km/h (110 mph) speed, 274 km (170 miles) range, 2.5 hours flying time, 4,876 m, (16,000 ft) ceiling and very light service load. Observance of the limitations was to be monitored by the Inter-Allied Military Control Commission.

Undeterred by these limitations, two sectors of German aviation quietly began to develop under the auspices of the Allied Commission. Firstly, one of von Seeckt's nominated officers in the *Fliegerzentrale* and former World War aviator, *Hptm.* Kurt Student, did everything he could to promote and generate interest in the sport of gliding. As head of von Seeckt's semi-covert *Technisches Amt (Luft)* in the *Heereswaffenamt* (Army Ordnance Office), Student was able to rally support among some of Germany's wartime pilots and the first gliding competitions were held on the Wasserkuppe – a high point in the Rhön Mountains in Hessen, north of Gersfeld – in the summer of 1921. These were to ignite the first sparks in what would eventually be a rushing flame of interest in sporting aviation in Germany. Over the next few years some of the best minds in German aviation participated in the Rhön competitions; Wolfgang Klemperer, Willy Messerschmitt, Kurt Student, Anthony Fokker, Ludwig Prandtl and Theodor von Kármán.

Secondly, following the war, and aided in part by the lightness of the limitations/definitions on the manufacture of civil aircraft, Professor Hugo Junkers had formed an aircraft company at Dessau and had built the Junkers F-13 all-metal, six-seat monoplane transport which had first flown on 25 June 1919 – three days before the signing of Treaty of Versailles. In 1921, Junkers had established their own transport airline, Junkers-Luftverkehrs AG which, amongst other accomplishments, carried out valuable and pioneering exploratory flights to China.

In 1922, Ernst Heinkel formed an aircraft manufacturing company at Warnemünde on the Baltic Coast followed the same year by *Dr.-Ing*. Claudius Dornier who built up his company from the old Zeppelin-Werke Lindau at Friedrichshafen. Two years later, Heinrich Focke and Georg Wulf founded the Focke-Wulf Flugzeugbau at Bremen and in 1926, the Bayerische Flugzeugwerke was founded at Augsburg from the remnants of the Udet-Flugzeubau (this would become Messerschmitt AG in 1938).

Perhaps the most astounding fact was that by the time the Paris Air Agreement of 1926 loosened the shackles that bound the manufacture of civil aircraft, Germany already possessed an efficient aircraft industry which had kept pace with current technical developments and which was maintaining a rate of production as high as that of any other European country.

RIGHT: Photographed at Berlin-Döberitz in 1919, these Fokker D VIII monoplane fighters and a single Fokker D VII bi-plane were operated by the last Jagdstaffel to survive before being destroyed to comply with the Treaty of Versailles. It was perhaps fitting that the first fighter squadron to be formed in the clandestine Luftwaffe was established at Döberitz.

RIGHT: Kurt Student was born in 1890 joining the army in 1910. Three years later he transferred to a military flight school and later led Jasta 9 and Jagdgruppe 3 during the First World War. He served with the Reichswehr after the conflict, transferring to the Luftwaffe in 1933 where he commanded the Technical School at Jüterbog. Between August 1935 and October 1936 he commanded the experimental station at Rechlin and became Inspector of the Paratroops in September. He is perhaps best known for leading the parachute assaults on the Low Countries in 1940 and on Crete a year later.

ABOVE: By 1935 a series or hangars and approach roads were built for the Rhön trials on the Wasserkuppe. This aerial view gives an idea of the extent of these buildings.

BELOW: A trainee pilot prepares to be catapulted into the air in an SG 38 glider. The aircraft carries the code D-4-719 in small digits on the lower part of the rudder which indicated that it was the 719th glider registered within Luftsport-Landesgruppe 4 headquartered in Berlin-Kurmark.

ABOVE: The Junkers J 10 (or CL.I as it had been known in the German Air Service) was an all-metal two seat attack monoplane which was later converted to civilian use by the addition of a canopy over the rear seat. Photographed on 12 March 1919, this aircraft, still in military markings, opened a regular service between Dessau and Weimar during that month.

LEFT: The famous Dutch aircraft designer, Antony Herman Gerhard Fokker, was born in Java in 1890. His company produced some of the best fighters used by the German Air Service during the First World War. This photograph was taken in 1922. In fact many of the company's aircraft were designed by Reinhold Platz who had joined Fokker as a welder in 1912. Fokker himself died on 23 December 1939 in New York, his body being buried at Haarlem in the Netherlands.

BELOW: During the summer of 1921 the first German gliding competitions were held on the Wasserkuppe – a high point in the Rhön Mountains in Hessen, north of Gersfeld. Here the well-known pioneer pilot, Wolfgang Klemperer, is at the controls of his "Blauen Maus" (Blue Mouse) glider on the Wasserkuppe in 1922. Klemperer was to improve the world duration record for gliders to 12 minutes on 30 August 1921.

LEFT: The young Willi Messerschmitt (left) and a French prisoner of war, pose in front of the S 5 glider at the Heidelstein, another gliding centre some 8 km from the Wasserkuppe. This photo was taken on 12 September 1915 long before Messerschmitt was to achieve world fame as an aircraft designer.

LEFT: Ernst Heinkel was born in 1888 at Grunbach in Wurttenburg, designing and building his first aircraft in 1911. Two years later he became chief designer of the Albatros company and in 1914, transferred to the Hansa Brandenburg Flugzeugwerke where he designed around forty different aircraft types. Following the First World War, he moved to Caspar, then on 1 December 1922 he formed his own company at Warnemünde on the Baltic coast. It was one of his aircraft, the He 51, which formed the initial equipment of many of the Luftwaffe's fighter units.

RIGHT: Prof. Dr. Claudius Dornier joined the Zeppelin Airship company in 1910, so impressing them that they allowed him to set up a separate research branch at Lindau for the design and construction of aeroplanes embodying his highly original theories. The first of these to be completed was the large multi-engined Rs I which was the first German aircraft to employ metal in its construction. His company then produced a variety of successful flying boats culminating in the Wal of 1922. Like many of his contemporary designers, Dornier was to establish a subsidiary abroad to build his designs, first in Italy, then in Switzerland.

BELOW: Prof. Heinrich Focke was born on 8 October 1890, he and his older brother, Wilhelm patenting a design for a pusher type aeroplane in December 1908. In 1909, the brothers were joined by Georg Wulf, producing their first successful aircraft, the A 5, in 1912. Following the construction of the A 7, Focke in conjunction with Wulf and Dr. Werner Naumann, formed the Focke-Wulf Flugzeugbau. Although the company was reasonably successful it was not until Kurt Tank became chief designer that it achieved its greatest success.

BELOW: Apart from his skill as a pilot, Udet and three others were also to establish an aircraft manufacturing company in 1922. The most successful design produced by the company was the U 12 Flamingo, a two-seat primary trainer powered by a 80 hp Siemens Sh 11 radial. This aircraft, a U 12a, number 48, had a smaller fin and rudder than the standard production machine.

ABOVE: Ernst Udet stands in front of his Albatros D Va in late 1917 as commander of Jasta 37. The letters applied to the aircraft fuselage – "LO" – were a reference to his fiance, Eleonore Zink.

ABOVE: Georg Wulf standing in the cockpit of the Siemens Sh 10 powered A 7 Storch designed by Heinrich Focke. Only one prototype of this two-seat trainer was completed but it was instrumental in prompting a group of Bremen businessmen to provide the capital to allow the establishment of the Focke-Wulf company. Wulf, who was to become an accomplished pilot, was killed on 29 September 1927 when the unusual F 19 Ente suddenly spun into the ground and was destroyed.

LEFT: Prof. Hugo Junkers was born on 3 February 1859, forming the Junkers company at Dessau for the manufacture of gas fired boilers, heating and ventilation equipment in 1895. He first became interested in aviation in 1909, being convinced that sheet metal construction could be applied to aircraft. In 1915 he built the J 1, the world's first all-metal aircraft which was nicknamed the "Tin Donkey". Despite its weight, the J 1 was faster than any of its contemporaries. The company continued with a series of successful metal aircraft including the F 13, the first all-metal airliner. Junkers died in 1935.

LEFT: The Junkers F 13 was one of the most important transport aircraft ever produced. An all-metal low wing monoplane with provision for four passenger seats, the aircraft pioneered the formula which became the norm for all subsequent airliners. This aircraft (W.Nr.531) is supposed to have received the first German civil registration D 1 in 1919. However, this was probably not applied until much later, the original D 1 possibly having been allocated to a Heinkel He 5.

"I had always dreamed of flying..."

FRITZ LOSIGKEIT

Fritz Losigkeit was one of the *Jagdwaffe's* most experienced unit commanders. His service career included duty with the *Legion Condor* and command positions with JG 26, JG 1 and as *Geschwaderkommodore* of JG 51. In the last weeks of the war he was posted to command JG 77. He was awarded the *Ritterkreuz* in April 1945 and attained a tally of 68 confirmed aerial victories during the course of 750 missions, including 13 kills on the western front. However, the story of his entry into the fighter arm is typical of many young pre-war pilots who had been tempted into the *Luftwaffe* by the thrill of glider flying and the glamour of powered flight. For Losigkeit however, aviation also offered a foil to the memories of harder times. As he recalls:"I was born in Berlin on 17 November 1913 during the rule of *Kaiser* Wilhelm II. I can remember very clearly the final year of the First World War because of the anxiety and hunger that we felt in the capital. My grandparents had a farm in East Prussia and they tried to send us some food, but very few of the packages reached us – most of them being destroyed or stolen because of the general strike which paralysed the city. I remember the tears that we cried because of these problems and I remember the great mood of revolution which was felt in Berlin at that time. When my father returned from the front, he told us stories of street fighting and combat... The position of the German Republic was very precarious and in May 1919, Friedrich Ebert became Provisional President of the German Reich. By that time, I had started school and was already facing up to living under spiralling inflation; though father may have earned money during the morning, it had virtually no value by the evening.

"I completed my *Abitur* on 3 March 1933 but shortly before that, on 30 January 1933, the NSDAP had won a majority in parliament and Hitler became *Reichskanzler.* This was a time of world-wide crisis that could quickly and most certainly influence our destiny.

"I had always dreamed of flying. Ever since I was a schoolboy I wanted to be a pilot. I built many types of model aircraft. During 1927-1928, Ernst Udet dazzled both Germany and the rest of the world with his aerobatic stunt flying. In 1927, Charles Lindbergh crossed the Atlantic non-stop in an aircraft. I bought all the books I could find on Otto Lilienthal, von Richthofen as well as any accounts on the ocean-crossing exploits of Köhl, Hünefeld and Fitzmaurice.

"But of one thing, I was sure; I wanted to become a pilot. In 1930 I had learned to fly gliders with the *Ring Deutscher Flieger* (German Aero Club) at Gatow, near Berlin. Slowly but surely, one began to hear a familiar declaration on the lips of the people – "Germany will fly again!" In fact, few people knew that as early as 1922, Germany and Russia had signed the Rapello Treaty which permitted some 120 German pilots to train as fighter pilots at Lipezk, a specially built air base 230 km from Orel. A friend of my father told me:"If you want to become a military aviator, join the *Landespolizei* (regional police). It will almost certainly be taken over by the *Reichswehr* in the near future."

"This was by no means certain, but I wanted to risk it and I knew that they already had aircraft and pilots. Because our army was not permitted to have pilots, I volunteered to join the *Landespolizei* as a Warrant Officer and on 20 April 1934, I was posted to the *Landespolizei* school in Brandenburg/Havel. Then later, whilst at the Potsdam/Eiche military academy, the officer section was taken over by the *Luftwaffe* and I attained the rank of *Fahnenjunker-Unteroffizier.* Having successfully completed the course, I was posted on 1 January 1936 to pilot school at Ludwigslust and then to Neuruppin where I obtained my A, B and C certificates. Our instructors there were mainly former *Lufthansa* men.

"On 1 April 1936, I was made a *Leutnant* in the *Luftwaffe* and was posted as one of the first qualified military pilots to an observer's school at Tutow. It was said that the future of military aviation lay in long-range bombing, but this type of flying did not appeal to me particularly. I wanted to become a fighter pilot.

"On 15 October 1936, I finally accomplished my dreams; I was posted to *2. Staffel, Jagdgeschwader* 132 "Richthofen" at Döberitz. My *Staffelkapitän* was the well-known 1936 Olympics champion, Gotthard Handrick. I also met and came to know such men as Adolf Galland, Walter Oesau, Herbert Ihlefeld and Wolfgang Schellmann all of whom would become well-known aces. From that point on, our primary mission was to fly. We flew as long as the weather permitted. We learned – and developed – different fighter tactics (later, fighter pilot trainees would learn in dedicated *Jagdschulen* or Fighter Schools, but at that time, they did not exist). The first fighter instructors nearly all came from Döberitz."

LEFT: Following the establishment of the Rhön gliding competitions on the Wasserkuppe in 1921, some of the best minds in German aviation technology were involved including Prof. Dr.-Ing. Ludwig Prandtl who pioneered airflow development at the University of Göttingen. He later founded the Aerodynamische Versuchsanstalt am Kaiser-Wilhelm Institute. His approach and pioneering research methods were later adopted by other countries in carrying out Aerodynamic Studies.

RIGHT: Prof. Theodor von Kármán was another pioneer aviator and designer to develop his skills in the Rhön gliding competitions. Other famous persons to sponsor the competitions were Prinz Heinrich of Prussia and General Ludendorff.

LEFT AND ABOVE: Those who saw Ernst Udet's flying displays will never forget the skill shown by the First World War fighter ace, whose score of 62 victories was second only to von Richthofen in the German Air Service. One of his most spectacular stunts was to pick up a piece of cloth from the ground with the wingtip of his aircraft. In these photographs, Udet is seen performing a joint stunt with a motor-racing car and motorcycle at the Eibsee and also touching the grass during a low-speed, wing-tip "skid" at Tempelhof.

Udet U 12a (Spezial)
As flown by Ernst Udet during the early 1930s.
This aircraft was constantly modified and repainted
and the profile shows it in one of its many guises.

Detail of sponsorship badge

Auto Union
Möbiloel

RIGHT: Two of the finest aerobatic pilots of their generation, Ernst "Udlinger" Udet (left) and Willi Stör at the Deutsche Verkehrsfliegerschule (DVS) or Commercial Pilots School at Schleissheim.

ABOVE: The Udet 12a (Spezial) powered by a Siemens Sh 11 engine. This aircraft, carrying the civil registration D-822, was re-painted several times, with the predominant colour always being bright red.

LEFT: A starboard side view of D-822 showing yet another modification to the colour scheme. This machine was used by Udet in his flying displays at Cleveland, Ohio in 1931 and Los Angeles, California in 1932

LEFT: An aerial view of the training centre at Lipezk. When the centre was first taken over by the Germans, it had one hangar, a workshop, an old factory shed for supplies and an administration building. By the summer of 1925, a second runway, new hangars, repair depots, an engine test-bed, barracks, medical quarters and a rail connection to the nearby station had been completed.

ABOVE: A dubious greeting warned new recruits at Lipezk of the harsh conditions they could expect at the clandestine training centre: "*A Hearty Welcome to the Arse of the World*".

BELOW: Arranged in two neat rows, these Udet U 12 a Flamingos were operated by the DVS at Schleissheim near München. From April 1927, the DVS began training new, young pilots or "Jungmärkern". After a year's instruction the pilots earned their B-2 certificates having passed the commercial pilot's course.

ABOVE: During 1925 a First World War fighter pilot, Theo Croneiss, director of Sportflug GmbH, entered his Messerschmitt M 17 in several contests and was able to achieve great success. As a result, Messerschmitt (seen here to the right) and Croneiss (left) soon became firm friends and the latter was able to finance the establishment of the Messerschmitt Flugzeugbau GmbH at Bamberg.

"Welcome to the arse of the world..."

In 1922, representatives of the Allied powers met at what became known as the Conference of Genoa. During this conference, Britain and France endeavoured to persuade Russia to seek war reparation payments from Germany. The Reichs Chancellor, Joseph Wirth, realised that such a situation, if allowed to happen, could have severe consequences for Germany's struggling post-war economy and its attempts at rearmament. He began to make urgent recommendations that Germany and Russia should open bilateral negotiations. Thankfully for Germany however, the Conference of Genoa ended in stalemate and events moved extremely rapidly in the Germans' favour. At 1.15 a.m. on Easter Sunday morning, 16 April 1922, the Soviet representative, A.A.Ioffe, telephoned Baron Ago von Maltzen, the head of the German Foreign Ministry's Russian section. Astonishingly, by 6.30 p.m. that evening, while the British and French were "kicking their heels" in Genoa, Germany and Soviet Russia had signed the Treaty of Rapello, an accord which expressly freed Germany from any reparations payments to Russia and introduced a series of trade agreements between the two countries.

Soon after the ratification of the Treaty, and initiated largely by von Seeckt, certain secret military agreements were made between the German and Russian governments, which, ultimately, would hold significant benefits for the development of the German *Luftwaffe*. Russia had declared herself willing to place airfields and labour at the disposal of Germany for the testing of German aircraft and equipment. In return, Germany was to make available to the Russians the technical knowledge they had gleaned as a result of their test programmes as well as offering training to Russian airmen and soldiers.

The German military presence in Russia began in 1923 with a *Reichswehr* liaison office in Moscow which placed a number of German pilots and technicians at the disposal of the Red Air Force which was then still in an early stage of development. As a result of this aid, the Russians offered Germany use of the existing airbase at Odessa, but the *Reichsmarine* with its own facilities in Germany was not interested. Eventually, an airfield located at a place far from where the prying eyes of the Inter-Allied Aviation Commission could see was found. Following the signing of an agreement on 15 April 1925, a clandestine flying school and flight test centre was established near the spa town of Lipezk, some 500 km (310 miles) south-east of Moscow, close to the Voronezh River. Officially known as the *"Wissenschaftliche Versuchs-und Prüfanstalt für Luftfahrzeuge"* this was to be the first real training centre for the German Air Force since the First World War.

The field was already occupied by Russian personnel when the Germans arrived and operations by both sides were kept strictly apart. By the summer of 1925 following the completion of an extensive construction programme, the facility boasted two runways, a number of hangars, repair depots, a state-of-the-art engine test-bed, barracks, administration buildings, medical quarters and a rail connection to the nearby station at Lipezk. All this cost Germany RM 2 million per year.

All activity was carried out on a "civilian" basis, with the permanent instructors – many of them young graduate engineers – being recruited from *Lufthansa*, the German airline or contracted in from private flying schools in Germany.

The first two years were spent organising "refresher" courses for *"Altmärkern"* or veteran airmen, many of whom had flown in the First World War. Much of this was organised by the government-sponsored organisation known as "Sportflug GmbH" (lit. "Sport Flying Ltd") using airfields at Osnabrück, Schkeuditz, Schleissheim, Stettin and Würzburg. Although these schools were, outwardly, supposed to have been seen as "sports flying centres", their real purpose was to provide basic flying training to civilian and military personnel in readiness for service with the *Reichswehr*. From April 1927 however, the emphasis was on the training of new, young pilots or *"Jungmärkern"*. *"Jungmärkern"* underwent one year's training at a *Deutsche Verkehrsfliegerschule* (DVS) or Commercial Pilots School in Germany where they earned their B-2 certificates having passed the commercial pilot's course. The first such school had been established in 1925 – almost coinciding with the commencement of activities at Lipezk – at Berlin-Staaken. This school was intended to train pilots for the growing number of small commercial airlines which had been set-up in Germany following the First World War such as the Deutsche Luft Reederei, Deutscher Aero Lloyd, Aero Union AG (a Dornier venture) and Europa Union (Junkers). Very soon the *Reichswehr* realised that the Berlin-Staaken facility with its all-weather, blind-flying and navigational training equipment, was perfect for training military pilots. The demand on Staaken soon grew to a point where further such facilities were needed and in 1927, additional DVS schools were opened at Schleissheim and Braunschweig. Each year, the ten candidates from the DVS Schleissheim – which specialised in training fighter pilots – who showed the most promise and aptitude were sent to Lipezk for six months.

It is interesting to note that there were no bomber crew courses held at Lipezk, although some experiments in this area were conducted in 1928. The fighter training courses at the base reflected German Army attitudes at that time. According to contemporary doctrine, which essentially focused on air power providing tactical

LEFT: In the 1920s, Paul Bäumer, a fighter pilot who had gained the Pour le Mérite and 43 victories during the First World War, founded his own passenger airline in Hamburg. He is seen here in the cockpit of an Udet U 12a "Flamingo", D-714. This aircraft belonged to the DLV (Deutsche Luftfahrt Verband e.V.) the organisation of German flying clubs. Bäumer was killed near Copenhagen on 15 July 1927 when testing the Rohrbach Ro IX Rofix parasol wing fighter for the Turkish government.

RIGHT: This converted L.V.G. C VI of the airline Deutsche Luftreederei flew the first Berlin-Leipzig-Weimar service on 5 February 1919. At this time the aircraft was still wearing military camouflage and markings before the civil registration system was introduced.

LEFT: The first Deutsche Verkehrsfliegerschule (DVS) or Commercial Pilots School was established at Berlin-Staaken, but by 1927 the demand on this venue had grown to such a point that two additional DVS schools were opened at Schleissheim near München and Braunschweig. This aerial view shows the main hangar at Schleissheim.

support, the role of the fighter was confined purely to Army support by intercepting enemy aircraft at low- and medium-level over the battlefield and by entering dogfights with a view to neutralising enemy fighters.

This belief formed the basis for operational training at Lipezk from the summer of 1925, though from 1927, courses were also held for observers. Each course was comprised a *Jagdstaffel*, (fighter squadron), a *Beobachterstaffel* (observer squadron) and a *Jagdlehr-* or *Beobachterlehrstaffel* (fighter- and observer demonstration squadron).

Potential fighter pilots arrived at Lipezk in the summer (there were no courses during the winter), invariably welcomed by a sign that proclaimed: *"Herzlich Willkommen am Arsch der Welt"* – "A Hearty Welcome to the Arse of the World". By 1929, they usually stayed for 20 to 22 weeks during which time they worked through a comprehensive practical training programme and completed all items contained in the "Fighter Manual" such as tactics, operations and the principles of command. The practical side included air-drill regulations, formation flying in echelons of two or three aircraft, aerobatics, high-altitude flying, air-to-air and air-to-ground practice firing, bombing practice and mock combat, the latter item being regarded as the high spot of the course.

Mock combat involved two *"Staffeln"* of nine aircraft flying against each other in a "dogfight". Each aircraft was equipped with a gun camera and the resulting films were used to analyse strengths and weaknesses.

The tedium of living in such a bleak and primitive landscape as that found around "the arse of the world" was alleviated by the fighter pilots playing practical jokes on each other such as shaving heads to create the so-called *"Billiardkugel"* or "Billiard Ball" look and raising mock fire alarms during which certain supervisory personnel were accidentally "extinguished".

Relations with the Russians were generally good. German officers often participated in Russian troop manoeuvres held in the Voronezh area, thereby gaining a valuable insight into the employment of air forces in tactical military operations. A few mishaps did, inevitably, occur such as when a local peasant was shot and killed during an air-to-ground gunnery session and several locals were hit by fragments when a Fokker D XIII fighter trainer crashed and exploded.

Between 1925 and 1933, 125 fighter pilots and 100 navigators were trained at Lipezk under the supervision of 60-70 permanent German staff who reported to the base commander, *Major* Stahr, after whom, the *"Fliegerschule Stahr"* was named. A security leak in 1926 forced a review of operating methods and greater discretion in who was actually sent to Lipezk. All active-list officers were banned by the German government from attending courses and so it was "standard procedure" for them to resign their commission and travel to Lipezk on false documents. Upon completion of their course, such officers regained their commissions.

The most commonly used aircraft for fighter training was the Fokker D XIII and 18 such aircraft equipped the *Jagdstaffel* with a further 16 in reserve. The *Stab* was equipped with a Junkers F 13 and A 20, the *Beobachterstaffel* with four Heinkel HD 17s and several more Heinkel HD 17s, Albatross L 69s as well as one Fokker D VII and a Heinkel HD 21 were used for training.

The Fokker D XIII was essentially a re-engined and more powerful variant of the D XI, fifty of which had been ordered on behalf of the *Reichswehr* by the financier, Hugo Stinnes. It was intended that the D XIs would go to Lipezk, but the order was cancelled and the aircraft sold to Rumania in 1925. The D XIII was powered by a 570 hp Napier Lion XI 12-cylinder water-cooled engine. Retaining the twin 7.92 mm LMG 08/15 armament of the D XI, the D XIII first flew on 12 September 1924, at which time it was claimed to be the fastest fighter in the world. Eventual total production was limited to the fifty aircraft allocated for Lipezk. By 1 October 1929, 43 Fokker D XIIIs were on strength at Lipezk, these being serial numbers 4599-4601, 4603-4625, 4625, 4627, 4687-4690, 4698, 4700, 4702-4706 and 4865.

The task of transporting the Fokkers (and their spare parts and ancillary equipment) to *Flugzentrum Lipezk* (as it was later called) was achieved by moving them by water from Stettin to the base via Leningrad. The aircraft were described as "mail-planes" and the cockpit instructions were in Spanish in order to give the impression that they were part of an export order. In order to keep the whole process secret, movement of spares usually took place at night or in foggy weather, often placing the lives of those involved at risk. However, ultra-suspicious customs officials at Leningrad and Bigossovo invariably caused delays to supplies. Nevertheless, the value of what was taking place at Lipezk was considered important enough to justify both the risks and the delays. In fact, the Germans became quite ingenious and on at least one occasion managed to get the Napier Lion engines used on the Fokker D XIII to the makers works in England for repair and then back to Lipezk without being discovered!

Inevitably, accidents and crashes occurred and men lost their lives. On such occasions, the bodies of the unfortunate airmen were crated and smuggled out of Stettin described as machine parts.

Noteworthy is the fact that some of the pilots who attended the April-September 1932 course at Lipezk, which was to be one of the last, later went on to become famous and successful *Luftwaffe* day and night-fighter aces; Wolfgang Falck, Günther Lützow, Hannes Trautloft and Günther Radusch.

RIGHT: This camera gun film was taken at Lipezk during gunnery training. Many of the centre's aircraft had different coloured fins and rudders. For example, "White 41" flown by Max Ibel, had green and white vertical stripes. These two stills show Fokker D XIIIs "White 47" and "White 29". These machines have white fuselage bands.

Fokker D XIII
Flown by Max Ibel at Lipezk in the Soviet Union in 1932. Note the absence of national insignia and the brightly coloured vertical tail surfaces.

RIGHT: Walter Kroll seated in the cockpit of a Fokker D XIII fighter trainer at Lipezk. Like most German aircraft at Lipezk, his aircraft retained its natural plywood coloured wings and engine-turned metal engine cowling. The remainder of the fuselage, horizontal tail surfaces and wheel discs were painted dark green. Kroll's personal aircraft was number "White 8".

ABOVE: This Fokker D XIII carried the standard finish adopted by aircraft at "Fliegerschule Stahr" so-named after its first commander, Major Stahr. The aircraft, coded, "White 6", had a white chevron painted on both sides of the fuselage and the fin and rudder were painted in red and white horizontal stripes.

LEFT: A view of Lipezk airfield taken in 1933 shortly before the centre was dissolved. The view shows the triple hangar number 1.

"To our good friends in the USSR...!"

WOLFGANG FALCK

" **I** was born in Berlin on 19 August 1910 and, after my studies, I decided to enlist in the *Reichswehr,* several of my relations already having distinguished military careers. While serving as a officer cadet in the *Hirschberger Bataillon*, I heard that *Generaloberst* von Seekt was looking for volunteers to train for military aviation. With four of my comrades I decided to apply. After numerous tests only 30 of the original 52 applicants remained, but I was one of the lucky ones. We, the 30 "winners", were then sent to Schleissheim for a year to undergo basic pilot instruction. It was 1931.

"After about a year some comrades and I were selected to be sent to the Soviet Union to undergo fighter pilot training. Our small group of 16 men, ten from the Army *(Heer)* and six from the Navy *(Marine)*, then boarded a train in Berlin. The treaty between Germany and the Soviet Union being highly secret, we were dressed as civilians so that we could not be identified as soldiers. Our train left Germany in the direction of Torun (Thorn) and the Soviet border. The controls were quite stiff but our "guides" helped us greatly so that we passed through them without difficulty.

"When we arrived in Moscow we were greeted with a friendly welcome and soon transferred to Lipezk, in the Woronesh near Tambow. Our quarters were simple wooden barracks but we were well looked after and even had a tennis court. We began our training on Fokker D XIII fighters. At the facility I met Hannes Trautloft, Günther Radusch, Günther Lützow, Ralph von Rettberg and Ekkehard Hefter (who was killed on 28 September 1936 in Spain). We quickly made good friends with the local population, but our instructors were all German. All our aircraft and equipment also came from Germany. The agreement between our two governments allowed the Soviets to photograph and test any new aircraft or engines when they arrived before they were handed over to us.

"Our training was quite rigorous. I remember that during one low level training session two pilots collided and were killed. The day before our group departed, we had a gala dinner at Lipezk with some Soviet officers. I had the honour of proposing the toast for our session, exclaiming: *"To our great USSR friends!"* General Tukatchewsky (who was later executed by Stalin) raised his glass full of vodka, crying: *"In honour of great Germany..!"*

"When I returned to Germany after six months in Russia, I was briefly given command of a small army formation with the rank of *Leutnant*. Shortly afterwards I transferred Schleissheim where I became a flying instructor, and then moved to a newly formed *Jagdgruppe* under the command of Werner Junck, my former instructor at Lipezk. I did not stay with this unit for long because shortly afterwards I was transferred to *Jagdgeschwader Richthofen* as *Geschwaderadjutant*. On 1 July 1938 I took over command of the newly formed 8./JG 132 which was later successively renamed 5./JG 141 and 2./ZG 76."

LEFT: The Heinkel HD 17 two-seat reconnaissance aircraft was designed in 1924 by Ernst Heinkel. Powered by a British 450 hp Napier Lion engine, the aircraft had a maximum speed of 385 km/h (240 mph) at sea level. After an observer school was established at Lipezk in 1926, the type became the section's main equipment.

RIGHT: A line up of Fokker D XIIIs photographed at Lipezk. Most of the facility's aircraft were left in natural finish apart from the rear fuselage and horizontal tail which were painted dark green. All D XIIIs carried large white identification numbers on either side of the fuselage together with a white rear fuselage band or white chevron.

Fokker D XIII
One of the aircraft used at Lipezk in 1932. Often known as "Fliegerschule Stahr" after its first commander, Major Stahr, the school was established in 1925 and finally closed in 1933.

LEFT: The Fokker D XI was one of several types tested at Lipezk. The D XI was an improved version of the D IX which was in turn a development of the famous wartime D VII. Powered by a 300 hp Hispano-Suiza engine the aircraft had a maximum speed of 225 km/h (140 mph) some 30 km/h (20 mph) slower than the D XIII.

ABOVE: A group of trainee pilots being reviewed by Göring at the training school at Lipezk in Russia. From the right of the picture are Wolfgang Falck and Günther Radusch who were to become pioneer night fighter pilots in the Luftwaffe. Sixth from the right is Günther Lützow who later became Kommodore of JG 3 and the second Luftwaffe pilot to score 100 victories. To his right is Hannes Trautloft who was to lead JG 54 and, like the other three, was awarded the Ritterkreuz.

RIGHT: Experiments were carried out at Lipezk with a Fokker D XIII fitted with skis. "White 11", shown here taxying in the snow, had a white-painted fin and rudder. Douglas Pitcairn's aircraft, "White 14", had its fin and rudder painted in a blue and white diamond pattern. By 1 October 1929, 43 Fokker D XIIIs were on strength at Lipezk.

The Restoration of Power and the first fighter units

According to one official history of the *Luftwaffe,* by 1926 "Germany was already the most air-minded nation in Europe." Certainly, following negotiations between the German government and representatives of the other signatories to the Treaty of Versailles, the Paris Air Accords of May that year lifted some of the earlier limitations and definitions which had been imposed. Though the ban on military aircraft prevailed, the German aircraft industry was allowed to build, under inspection, aircraft which possessed fighter performance characteristics but which could only be used for flying competitions and record-breaking purposes.

This paved the way for a major expansion. Significant developments were taking place within the commercial air transport sector and in January of that year, the three surviving commercial airlines - Deutscher Aero Lloyd, Junkers Luftverkehrs AG and the Deutsch-Russische Luftverkehrsgesellschaft – merged to form a new national airline, Deutsche Lufthansa AG (DLH).

As its commercial director, DLH appointed the thirty-six year old Erhard Milch. Born in 1892 in Wilhelmshaven of Jewish ancestry, Milch had flown as an aerial observer during the First World War and after the war joined the East Prussian *Freikorps* for whom he formed a paramilitary air-police squadron at the former Zeppelin airfield of Seerappen in September 1919. When the Allies forced Germany to dissolve her air police squadrons in March 1921, Milch entered civilian life for the first time, joining the Lloyd Ostflug airline as head of their Danzig office. Over the next eight years, he progressed rapidly through the various tiers of airline management, quickly developing a reputation as a dynamic and hard-headed businessman. He successfully ran the Danzig Air Mail service for Junkers, negotiated Junkers expansion into the Polish market and travelled to America, a country which greatly impressed him.

Milch first met Adolf Hitler in 1930 and was extremely impressed with both the Nazi leader's understanding of the political and military potential of aviation as well as his attractive ideals of combined nationalism and socialism. Milch was also very aware of the growing strength of Hitler's appeal within Germany at the time and also of the threat which his Jewish ancestry posed to him, should Hitler and the Nazis seize power. By 1932, Milch had placed DLH aircraft at Hitler's disposal and arranged for RM 1,000 per month to be deposited into the personal bank account of the *Reichstag* President, Hermann Göring who frequently proclaimed support for DLH and supported its interests in the German political arena.

In January 1933, Hitler rose to power as German chancellor and two months later, recognising the tremendous propaganda value in sports flying, made moves to integrate the many private flying clubs throughout Germany into one unified organisation promoting national interest in gliding, aero-modelling, balloons and powered aircraft. From that point on, it became compulsory for anyone who wanted to fly to join the new Berlin-based *Deutsche Luftsportverband* (DLV). Göring, now *Reichsminister* for Aviation, appointed Bruno Loerzer, head of the DLV which comprised sixteen regional *Fliegerlandesgruppen.* Despite the fact that this was not – externally at least – a Nazi Party organisation, paramilitary style ranks and insignia were introduced along with civilian clothing which was cut in a military manner.

When in May 1933, Hitler appointed Milch Secretary of State of the new German Air Ministry, he commissioned a former business colleague of his, Dr Robert Knauss, to write a major study analysing the strategic concept of Germany's proposed new air force. Milch had met Knauss while both men had worked for Lufthansa, during the 1920s. Knauss too had served with the Imperial German Air Service as an observer during the First World War and had later taken part in pioneering long-range aeronautical expeditions from Germany to Istanbul, Baghdad and Peking. Knauss was a firm advocate of the principles espoused by the Italian air theorist, Giulio Douhet and, as such, in his report to Milch, he argued that only "strategic" bombing would allow the "restoration of Germany's great power position in Europe." Poland and especially France, he argued, would nevertheless resist such a move on Germany's

BELOW: In May 1933, Hitler appointed Erhard Milch Secretary of State in the new German Air Ministry. Milch had been born in 1892, being commissioned into an Imperial Army artillery regiment in 1909. In 1915 he transferred to the Air Service, where he flew reconnaissance operations until the end of the First World War. After that conflict he entered business, becoming director of Lufthansa, the German airline, in 1926. He is seen here wearing the uniform of the Deutsche Versuchsanstalt für Luftfahrt (German Research Institute for Aviation).

LEFT: This Junkers F 13 was photographed at Berlin-Templehof in 1921. Note the absence of hangars or administrative buildings at this time.

BELOW: Erhard Milch (centre) who became head of Deutsche Lufthansa when the airline was established in 1926. The aircraft in the background is a Junkers G 24 three-engined airliner a development of the F 13. During 1926 Lufthansa used two G 24s, D-901 and D-903, to fly from Berlin to Peking and back to test the possibilities of establishing a regular Far Eastern service.

ABOVE: A group of personalities from Deutsche Lufthansa pose with a Turkish flight engineer during the 1920s, following a return postal flight between Berlin and Baghdad. From left to right are: Bredow, Kreuger, Direktor Milch, Flugkapitän Klaus, Dr. Knauss, the Turkish flight engineer Fehmi Mehhed, Walter Angermund and von Gablenz. Dr Robert Knauss was later to write a major study analysing the strategic concept of Germany's air force, proposing the creation of an air force, whose decisive element would be a fleet of 400 long-range four-engined "strategic" bombers.

LEFT: The Junkers F 13a production aircraft was powered by a 185 hp BMW IIIa engine which gave it a crusing speed of 140 km/h (87 mph). This aircraft, registered D-410 (W.Nr. 740), was operated by Südwestdeutsche L.V. at Frankfurt am Main in 1925. It was destroyed in September of that month.

part which meant that Germany faced the very real prospect of a preventative war waged by these two powers against her. To overcome the military weakness from which Germany had suffered since 1918, Knauss proposed the rapid creation of a strong air force, whose decisive element would be a fleet of 400 long-range four-engine "strategic" bombers. These aircraft would be capable of attacking and destroying the many key "strategic" targets which lay within in an industrialised enemy's borders, thus crippling industrial productivity and striking terror into major centres of population. With such a force on hand, Germany would be able to retaliate against Poland and France and with this knowledge, these two countries would think twice before embarking on any strike against Germany.

Milch absorbed Knauss's recommendations and with characteristic energy, flair and ruthlessness, worked hard to improve and expand Germany's aircraft industry to such a level that a strategic bomber force could become a reality. In January 1933, the aircraft industry employed 4,000 workers but by the following year this had increased to 16,870 and by autumn 1938, to 204,100. Milch was also aware that Knauss's recommendations for a powerful bomber force received fundamental support from the intuitive and extremely capable Chief of the Air Command Office, *Generalleutnant* Walther Wever. However, Wever differed from Knauss on one essential point; as an ardent National Socialist he had read and digested the writings of Adolf Hitler in *Mein Kampf* in which the *Führer* wrote that a war of revenge against France or Britain was pointless. The real, strategic enemy was Russia and therefore, Wever, realised, the need was for a bomber with sufficient range to reach Russia's industrial heartland and beyond – as far as the Ural Mountains if necessary. Wever received support for his beliefs from other senior officers within the Air Ministry's Technical Office.

However, unlike Knauss, Wever also recognised the need for- and importance of developing a significant fighter force. Manoeuvres conducted during the winter of 1933-34 convinced Wever and others that a strategic bomber fleet alone would not necessarily destroy an enemy air force and that bombers would need protection in enemy airspace from escort fighters. The manoeuvres, which were based on a scenario envisaging a French invasion of south-west Germany, were well conceived and based on in-depth intelligence information on the French road and rail system and the French air force and airfield infrastructure. Wever made sure that all aspects of the German air force – from heavy bombers to dive bombers to transports – were somehow involved. The results proved to Wever that fighters would be needed to operate in the close interdiction and air support roles, attacking the enemy army directly. Furthermore, Wever knew that in a war of strategic bombing, it would be vital to defend Germany's cities against retaliation with squadrons of defensive fighters. Nevertheless because of the entrenched "bomber doctrine" which dominated German thinking, Milch's planned 1934-35 aircraft production programme allowed for 822 bombers (Do 11s, Do 23s and Ju 52s) and only 251 single engine fighters (Ar 64s, Ar 65s and He 51s).

Interestingly, in the spring of 1936, Wever brought together a group of officers from both the operational and organisational arms of the *Luftwaffe* with a view to conducting a detailed study into the employment of fighters in a proposed war against Czechoslovakia. Wever then invited Göring and the commanders in chief of both the Army and the Navy to discuss and evaluate the results. Such innovation on Wever's part served to open the senior command's eyes to the benefits of correctly deployed fighter aircraft.

Göring's initial intention had been to establish a fighter *Staffel* at Rechlin and to equip it with Italian Caproni CR 30s, but these aircraft were never delivered and the proposal came to nothing. Furthermore, in May 1933, Göring summoned some seventy young pilots - NCOs and a handful of civilian pilots, but all freshly qualified from the DVS at Schleissheim or other schools, to a meeting in Berlin. At this meeting, the *Reichsminister* announced that a special fighter training course was to be held in Italy run by the Italian Air Force and that the German pilots were to attend it.

Donning civilian clothes, the pilots travelled by various routes to Frankfurt-am-Main where they were subjected to a somewhat tedious three-day security lecture. It was intended that half the group were to train at Udine and the other half at Grotaglie.

In the group bound for Grotaglie was a young man named Adolf Galland who was destined to become intrinsically linked with the development and campaigns of the *Luftwaffe* as its famous and flamboyant *General der Jagdflieger* from December 1941 to January 1945. For his part, Galland remembered the course as a complete waste of time. Upon arrival in Italy, the Grotaglie group was hurried into barracks and locked up. They were then presented with worn-

ABOVE: One of the most beautiful aircraft of the between war period, the He 70 was designed by the Günter brothers as a fast transport. The first passenger carrying He 70s were used by Deutsche Lufthansa on its Berlin-Hamburg-Köln-Frankfurt am Main service, and later other routes inside Germany. With the birth of the Luftwaffe, two military versions were produced, the He 70 E and F, these being tested as fighter, reconnaissance and bombing aircraft.

ABOVE AND RIGHT: Two views of He 111 C-04, D-ABYE "Königsberg" which was delivered to Lufthansa in the summer of 1936. The aircraft could carry ten passengers at a maximum speed of 315 km/h (196 mph) but was considered by the airline to be too expensive for commercial operation. Nevertheless by the summer of 1937 the type was operating on no fewer than 16 routes.

LEFT: The He 111 V16, D-ASAR, had straight wings similar to those later fitted to the H-series bomber widely used by the Luftwaffe. The aircraft was used by Erhard Milch as his personal transport.

out uniforms which had formerly belonged to Italian Air Force officer candidates. There they remained, in clean conditions but under constant observation, for two months. Without sight of a female, pretending to be south Tyrolean recruits and with light-fingered Italian orderlies to attend to them, the Germans endured a very frustrating and trying time.

Galland also remembered the training to be "grossly inadequate". The Italians had assumed that their German charges knew virtually nothing about flying. Eventually however, each pilot managed to achieve some 60 hours flying under some good Italian instructors. Nevertheless, this did not stop Galland and his fellow pilots from returning to Germany in September 1933, "... disillusioned and sunburned."

As early as July 1933, a document signed by Milch had proposed the formation of "*Jagdgeschwader Eins*" (Fighter Wing One) with six *Staffeln* or Squadrons plus a "*Seejagdstaffel Eins*" (Naval Fighter Squadron One). The idea for the formation of the former unit, which was to take place at Rechlin, was abandoned around 1 October 1933. By this time, however, three *Reklamestaffeln* - literally "Propaganda Squadrons" had been established as clandestine fighter units. The three squadrons were: *Reklamestaffel Ostdeutschland* at Neuhausen near Königsburg, *Reklamestaffel Mitteldeutschland* at Berlin-Staaken and *Reklamestaffel Süddeutschland* at Fürth near Nürnberg.

On 1 April 1934, the second two *Reklamestaffeln* were transferred to Döberitz near Berlin where they were to eventually form the nucleus of the *Luftwaffe's* first fighter *Gruppe*, I./JG 132. This unit was commanded by *Major* Robert von Greim, the former First World War *Pour le Mérite* holder. Von Greim had commanded *Jagdgruppe* 9 and had ended the war with 26 confirmed aerial victories. He later became one of the architects of Chiang Kai-shek's Nationalist Air Force in China during the 1920s.

Long before the existence of the *Luftwaffe* was revealed to the public, another top secret document had been issued proposing the formation of two fighter *Regimente* (Regiments) each containing three *Gruppen* (Groups). These, and their proposed bases were:

Jagdregiment Döberitz	I. Gruppe	Döberitz
	II. Gruppe	(Jüterbog-Damm)
	III. Gruppe	(Zerbst area)
Jagdregiment Hamm	I. Gruppe	(Hamm area)
	II. Gruppe	(Unna area)
	III. Gruppe	(area west of Hamm)

These two regiments were eventually to become JG 132 and JG 134 respectively.

After the existence of the *Luftwaffe* was officially revealed to the world on 1 March 1935, six Regional Air Commands or *Luftkreiskommando* were created a month later. These *Luftkreis*, to which 15 Air Offices or *Luftamter* were subordinated, were territorial areas of command. The six Regional Air Commands , their headquarters and commanders were:

Luftkreiskommando I	Königsberg	Gen.Lt. Wochenfeld
Luftkreiskommando II	Berlin	Gen.Lt. Kaupisch
Luftkreiskommando III	Dresden	Gen.Maj. Schweickhardt
Luftkreiskommando IV	Münster	Gen.Lt. Halm
Luftkreiskommando V	München	Gen.Lt. Eberth
Luftkreiskommando VI	Kiel	Konteradmiral Zander

At this time three fighter squadrons were available, I./JG 132 (comprising the *Gruppe Stab*, 1 and *2. Staffel*) and *1./Küstenjagdgruppe* 136 (previously called "*Fliegerstaffel* (J) 1") at Kiel-Holtenau. Equipped with Arado Ar 65 and Heinkel He 51 single-seat fighters, this first fighter unit was given its three-digit designation of *Jagdgeschwader* "132" using the standard nomenclature of the time; the first digit "1" representing the units' number in its allocated *Luftkreis;* the second digit "3" signifying the type of unit it was, in this case "3" = fighters; the third digit "2" was the number of the *Luftkreis*. The *Gruppenstab* was established on 1 May 1934 with its associated three *Staffeln* forming up from 1 July.

On 14 March 1935, the JG 132 was bestowed the honourary title "*Richthofen*" in memory of the legendary First World War fighter ace, Manfred von Richthofen. The award of this title was symbolic of the importance the infant *Luftwaffe* placed on remembering its old heroes, for it had been on 20 May 1918 that the *Luftstreitkräfte* had redesignated *Jagdgeschwader* I, "*Jagdgeschwader Freiherr von Richthofen Nr.I*". On 19 March 1935, JG 132 performed a fly-past

LEFT: This Habicht glider was painted in the familiar overall pale cream finish used by most NSFK gliders, and carries the code D-4-1062 which indicates that it was the 1062 glider registered to Luftsport-Landesgruppen 4 with its headquarters in Berlin.

RIGHT: Erwin Teske at the controls of his Granau Baby. This aircraft carries the glider marking of the time: "D" = Deutschland, "4" = Luftsport-Landesgruppe 4 in Berlin and "827" = the aircraft's individual number. The emblem below the cockpit is that of the NSFK (National Sozialistische Flieger Korps) - the Nazi organisation responsible for training young German airmen.

LEFT: In October 1937 the DLV was replaced by the NSFK, a branch of the Nazi Party formed to encourage boys from 12 years old to take up flying. The NSFK was divided into seventeen administrative Luftsport-Landesgruppen, their gliders carrying a special registration system. The Minimoa glider seen here on the Wasserkuppe, carried the registration D-4-765. The letter "D" was for Deutschland or Germany with the first number directly indicating the Landesgruppe to which it was attached, in this case Gruppe 4 from Prussia with its headquarters in Berlin. The second series of numbers were allocated from a progressive list.

RIGHT: The NSFK had its own colour chart with six different shades which were to be used to paint its gliders. The colours were FAS 1, the pale cream, FAS 2, a medium blue, FAS 3, a medium brown, FAS 4, a light green, FAS 5, a chrome yellow and FAS 6, a medium grey. All NSFK gliders were painted in a basic scheme of pale cream (FAS 1) overall, but the Habicht (Hawk) shown here has a "sunburst" pattern luf medium blue (FAS 2) on the uppersurfaces of the wings. This glider, which belonged to Landesgruppe 15 headquartered at Stuttgart, also had the Olympic rings painted on the fuselage nose for the 1936 Olympic Games held in Berlin.

over Berlin, publicly disregarding and invalidating the Allied prohibitions on formation flying, particularly over towns and cities. On the 28th, Hitler, Göring and several high-ranking officials from the *Reichsluftfahrtministerium* (RLM) and the NSDAP visited Döberitz to attend the ceremonial naming of the unit.

Around this time a second *Gruppe* was added to JG 132 with its home base at Jüterbog-Damm some 70 km (45 miles) south of Berlin. As the *Luftwaffe's* first fighter unit, the *Richthofen Geschwader* was tasked with testing weaponry and equipment, I./JG 132 assigned to evaluating equipment and ground organisation matters, whilst II./JG 132 concentrated on tactics.

By 1 April 1936, a second *Geschwader*, JG 134, had been established with a nucleus provided by JG 132. At this time, most *Luftwaffe* units were formed by splitting older units in the so-called "*Mutter und Tochter*" procedure. The *Stab* and I. Gruppe of JG 134 were established at Dortmund, whilst the II. Gruppe formed up at Werl and the III. Gruppe at Lippstadt. On Hitler's 47th birthday, 20 April 1936, the *Geschwader* was accorded the honour title "*Horst Wessel*" after the young Berlin SA leader who became a venerated martyr of the Nazi movement following his death in a street brawl in the capital six years earlier.

The Stab, I./JG 134 and II./JG 134 received Ar 65s and Ar 68Es, whilst III./JG 134 was equipped with He 51s and Ar 68 Fs under *Hptm.* Oskar Dinort, the future *Kommodore* of *Stukageschwader 2 "Immelmann"*. On 9 March 1936, the Stab, 8. and 9./JG 134 moved to Köln-Butzweilerhof following the remilitarisation and occupation of the Rhineland, while 7./JG 134 transferred to Düsseldorf the same night. Their aircraft each carrying 1,000 rounds of ammunition, but without having undergone any preliminary gun and sight harmonisation, Dinort and his men circled over the cathedral in Köln around midday, landing at Butzweilerhof shortly afterwards. However, with its newly-trained pilots, the unit possessed little real offensive or defensive military value.

The origins of a third *Geschwader*, JG 136, actually pre-dated both JG 132 and JG 134. As has been mentioned previously, "*Fliegerstaffel (J) 1 Kiel-Holtenau*" – named after the old naval aviation barracks in which that unit was temporary based – had grown from the *Seejagdstaffel Eins*. This had, in turn, been formed on or around 1 October 1934 under the command of *Hptm.* Hermann Edert. By 1 April 1935 it had become 1.(*Küstenjagdstaffel*)/136. A second Squadron, 2.(*Küstenjagdstaffel*)/136, was formed on 1 April 1935, followed by 3.(*Küstenjagdstaffel*)/136 in September 1936. Together, these three *Staffeln* officially formed the First Gruppe of JG 136 and from 30 October 1936 the title "*Küstenjagdstaffel*" was dropped in favour of "*Jagdstaffel*". The unit was equipped with a mixture of Heinkel HD 38s, Ar 64s, Ar 65s and He 51s, this latter type intended to eventually replace all other types.

The nucleus of another fighter *Geschwader* was established at Bernburg on 1 April 1936 when I./JG 232 was created from a nucleus provided by II./JG 132. The unit was often known as "*Gruppe Loerzer*" after its *Kommandeur, Oberst* Bruno Loerzer. Like many units of the period, I./JG 232 was equipped initially with training aircraft such as the He 72 and Fw 56, but soon began to receive the He 51.

As we have seen, during the late 1920s and early 1930s, the *Deutsche Verkehrsfliegerschule* (DVS) Schleissheim assumed responsibility for the preliminary training of fighter pilots. On 1 April 1934, the school became officially known as the *Jagdfliegerschule* Schleissheim changing its name again exactly one year later to the "*Fliegergruppe (S) Schleissheim*" by which it was known until its eventual reorganisation as a A/B school. Finally, in 1939 it became *Jagdfliegerschule (JFS) 2 Schleissheim*. During the second half of 1935, Schleissheim was known to have operated Ar 64s, Ar 65s, Ar 66s, Fw 56s, He 45s and He 50s.

ABOVE: Adolf Hitler shakes hands with the Commander-in-Chief of the Luftwaffe, Generalfeldmarschall Hermann Göring. Born on 12 January 1893 at Rosenheim in Bavaria, Göring served with distinction as a fighter pilot during the First World War. After the war, he joined the Nazi Party, his fame as a fighter pilot and his qualities of leadership soon making him commander of the SA - Sturm Abteilung or Storm Troops. His involvement and injury in the Beer Hall Putsch of November 1923 led to his exile until 1926. He then became a deputy in the Reichstag in 1928, and President of that body after the Nazis' electoral success in 1932. He was appointed to lead the Luftwaffe in 1935. In 1938 he was promoted to Generalfeldmarschall and to Reichsmarschall in 1940.

BELOW: Bruno Loerzer, head of the DLV (Deutsche Luftsportverband), at the left of this photo, talking to Wolfgang Späte (right) at the 1935 Rhön trials on the Wasserkuppe. When the new German Air Ministry was established on 11 March 1933, Göring, then Reichsminister for Aviation, appointed his good friend Loerzer, Commissioner for Airships and head of the DLV (Deutsche Luftsportverband). During the First World War he had been awarded the Pour le Mérite as commander of JG 3, scoring 41 aerial victories. Loerzer was later to become commander of I./JG 232 and JG 334 in the new Luftwaffe. Späte, who was at this time one of Germany's best known glider pilots, eventually joined 5./JG 54 on the Eastern Front, becoming its Staffelkapitän in the autumn of 1941. In July 1942 he was transferred to the Rechlin Experimental Station where he formed Erprobungskommando 16 responsible for developing the Me 163 rocket fighter.

1933-1936

BELOW: A formation of Do 23 G bombers of 4./KG 153 in flight near Fürstenwalde in 1937. The code of the nearest Dornier to the camera, 32+K24, indicated that it was individual aircraft "K" of the fourth Staffel, "4", of the second Gruppe, "2", of the second Geschwader, "2", formed within Luftfkreiskommando 3, "3".

ABOVE: Early trials with the Do 11 were to show that the flying characteristics of the aircraft were far from perfect. Under certain conditions the wings vibrated alarmingly, necessitating the redesign of both the wing and enlargement of the vertical tail surfaces. The resulting variant, the Do 11 D seen here, was better, although problems with the retractable undercarriage were such that the unit was locked down on all service aircraft.

BELOW: The Heinkel HD 38 was the predecessor of the He 51 which was to equip many of the Luftwaffe's early fighter units. Two main variants were built, the HD 38a landplane and the HD 38b, c and d floatplanes. Powered by a 750 hp BMW VI engine, the HD 38a had a maximum speed of 292 km/h (181 mph) at sea level and carried an armament of two 7.9 mm machine-guns.

BELOW: Luftwaffe bomber crews are prepared for a training sortie in front of a Do 23. The Do 23 carried a crew of four; pilot, navigator, radio operator, bomb aimer/nose gunner and dorsal gunner and a defensive armament of three 7.9 mm machine-guns. Note that one of the 750 hp BMW VI twelve cylinder in line engines with its huge four-blade wooden propeller is running up.

ABOVE: By the early 1930s, there were two major manufacturers producing fighters in Germany, Arado and Heinkel. The former had produced a number of biplane interceptors during the 1920s including the SD II, SD III and Ar 64. Although a thoroughly undistinguished design, the Ar 64 provided the basis for the first fighter type delivered to the clandestine Luftwaffe, the Ar 65. Powered by a 750 hp BMW VI engine, the aircraft had a maximum speed of 300 km/h (186 mph) and carried an armament of two 7.9 mm machine-guns.

ABOVE: Photographed at their home base at Gotha, these Do 23 G-1 bombers of 3./KG 253 "General Wever" carry the typical five-character code system which was introduced for all Luftwaffe aircraft in late 1935. Although retained until the beginning of the Second World War by bomber, reconnaissance and transport units, the need for rapid identification meant that the system for fighters was changed by September 1936.

ABOVE: During the late 1920s the Heinkel company produced its first fighter design, the HD 37 biplane. This was developed, via the HD 38 and HD 43 into the He 49 in which the talented Günter brothers first had a hand. This sleek-looking biplane fighter had a top speed of over 200 mph, hardly consistent with its published role of advanced trainer. The He 51, which first flew in May 1933, was an aerodynamically improved version of the He 49 and was soon to form the equipment of the first Luftwaffe fighter units. These photos show the fourth, fifth and first A-series production He 51s, respectively registered D-IJAY, D-IDIE and D-IQEE.

BELOW: With a roar from its BMW engine, a He 51 A-1 fighter taxies out to its take-off position. It is interesting to note that the wheel spats were often removed both on the He 51 and the Ar 68.

ABOVE: The He 51 A-01, the first of nine pre-production aircraft, left the assembly line at Warnemünde during the spring of 1934. Several of these aircraft were delivered to the Reklamestaffel Mitteldeutschland for evaluation. At this time, the aircraft carries the red, white and black band on the starboard side of the vertical tail surfaces with the black Hakenkreuz on a white circle over a red band on the port side.

ABOVE: Three of the nine pre-production batch He 51 A-0 series aircraft taking off. The nearest machine D-IQEE, also shown middle right, shows the standard port side tail markings of the time, a red band with the Hakenkreuz inside a white circle. All the pre-production machines were finished in silver coloured aluminium dope.

ABOVE: A line-up of He 51s prior to delivery to a Luftwaffe fighter unit. The aircraft still bear their civil registrations with the black, white and red rear tail band on the starboard side of the vertical tail surfaces.

BELOW: Ground crews prepare a Staffel of He 51 fighters for a training sortie. At this time the aircraft, probably belonging to the Reklamestaffel Mitteldeutschland, had the black, white and red national insignia band painted across the fin and rudder. The other side of these surfaces would have had a red band painted in this position with a black Hakenkreuz superimposed on a white circle.

ABOVE: This picture taken at Döberitz near Berlin show He 51s of Reklamestaffel Mitteldeutschland being readied for operations. Note that the aircraft carry German civil registrations and black, white and red bands on the starboard side of their vertical tail surfaces.

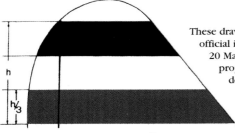

These drawings taken directly from the official instruction document dated 20 March 1934, show the standard proportions and measurement details of both the port and starboard tail markings.

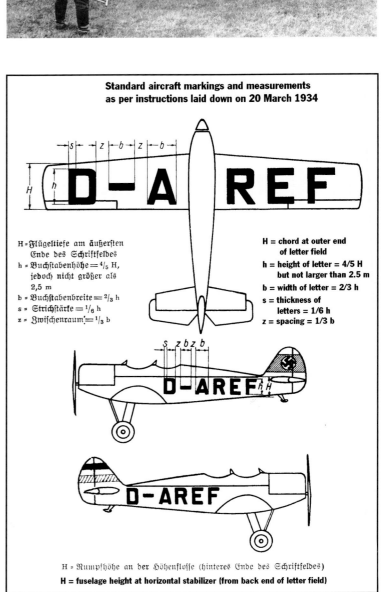

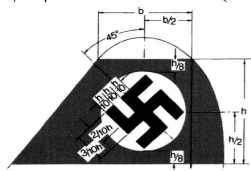

BELOW: By the autumn of 1933 three Reklamestaffeln - literally "Publicity Squadrons" had been established in Germany as clandestine fighter units. The three squadrons were: Reklamestaffel Ostdeutschland at Neuhausen near Königsburg, Reklamestaffel Mitteldeutschland at Berlin-Staaken and Reklamestaffel Süddeutschland at Fürth near Nürnberg. On 1 April 1934, the second two Reklamestaffeln were transferred to Döberitz near Berlin where they were to eventually form the nucleus of the Luftwaffe's first fighter Gruppe, I./JG 132. This photo, which was taken during this period, shows the unit's aircraft.

Standard aircraft markings and measurements as per instructions laid down on 20 March 1934

H = Flügeltiefe am äußersten Ende des Schriftfeldes
h = Buchstabenhöhe = 4/5 H, jedoch nicht größer als 2,5 m
b = Buchstabenbreite = 2/3 h
s = Strichstärke = 1/6 h
z = Zwischenraum = 1/3 b

H = chord at outer end of letter field
h = height of letter = 4/5 H but not larger than 2.5 m
b = width of letter = 2/3 h
s = thickness of letters = 1/6 h
z = spacing = 1/3 b

H = Rumpfhöhe an der Höhenflosse (hinteres Ende des Schriftfeldes)
H = fuselage height at horizontal stabilizer (from back end of letter field)

Markings of Aircraft and Airships 29 August 1936
The following is a translation of part of Reichsgesetzblatt No. 78, Encl. No.1 to Paras. 4, 12 and 75 of LuftVO - Luftverkehrsvorschrift (Air Traffic Ordinance) published by Reichsgesetzblatt (Reich Government Gazette) on 29 August 1936.

1. National Markings and Registration

a) Civil Aircraft
German aircraft and airships carry the letter **"D"** as national marking, followed by a four-letter registration. *Reich* Air Minister may permit non-standard registrations for airships.

On aircraft, the national identification **"D"** and idividual registration is carried on both sides of the fuselage, in the space between the wings and the vertical stabilizer, on monoplanes also on the upper and lower wing surfaces, biplanes under the lower wing and top of upper wing.

Airships carry the markings on both sides of the hull at the point of its greatest diameter, in such a way as to be visible from the side as well as from the ground, also on top of the hull at right angles to the fuselage markings equidistant from both.

Markings are to be applied either in solid black characters on light background or in light characters on dark background in wipe resistant paint, always to be kept clearly visible. The national letter **"D"** is separated from the registration by a hyphen of a length similar to the thickness of a letter. The area covered by the markings has to take the form of a rectangle, taking care that it is not obscured by engines, struts, undercarriage or floats.

On aircraft, the minimum distance of the lettering from the leading and trailing edges at the wing's narrowest point to be at least one-sixth of the letter's size. On airships, the size of the hull characters one-twelfth of the circumference measured at the hull's greatest diameter, but not larger than 2.50 m.

Registered and licenced **"air trailers"** carry the national letter **"D"** as stated above for powered aircraft .

Free balloons carry the national letter followed by the individual name in correspondence with the regulations for airships' lettering.

A Bücker Bü 131 showing an example of non military markings but operated by the Luftwaffe. The letter "D" being replaced by "WL".

fin's leading edge is open at the top.

The diameter of the white circle is three-quarters of the width of the red band (see Fig.2).

Length of the centre arms of the *Hakenkreuz* is half the width of the red band. Thickness of the arms of the *Hakenkreuz* and their distance from each other is one-tenth of the width of the red band.

Airships carry the *Reich* and national flag on both sides of the vertical stabilizers. Size of the flag is determined by the Air Ministry from case to case.

Sailplanes carry the *Reich* and national flag as described for powered aircraft.

Free balloons fly the *Hakenkreuz* flag.

Aircraft on which standard markings cannot be applied due to peculiarities of their construction or for other reasons will receive modified markings authorised by the Air Minister.

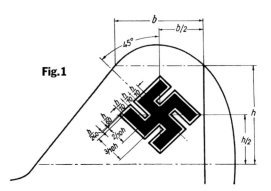

Fig.1

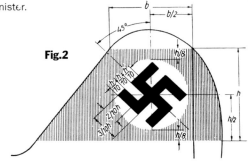

Fig.2

b) *LUFTWAFFE* AIRCRAFT
(1) All *Luftwaffe* aircraft carry the *Hakenkreuz* in place of the reich National flag.
1. dimensions of *Hakenkreuz* (see Fig.1)
2. white borderline of *Hakenkreuz* 1/4 of the thickness of the Hakenkreuz.
3. the white borderline is outlined by a black (colour 22) surround of a thickness 1/4 of the borderline.

(2) On aircraft with **non-military markings** operated by operational units, flying schools and other *Luftwaffe* organisations, the national letter **"D"** is replaced by **"WL"**, the other four registration letters remaining unchanged.

2. *Reich* and National Flag

Aircraft and **air trailers** carry the *Reich* and national flag in colour on both sides of the vertical fin, of equal size on both sides. Minimum size is half the height of the fin above the horizontal stabilizer. Length and height of the two flag bands should be in a 3:5 ratio.

The flag is applied as follows:
A black *Hakenkreuz*, angled at 45°, in a white circle on a red band, all possessing a common centre. The arms of the *Hakenkreuz* nearest to the

RIGHT: Facsimile of an official document giving details regarding the registration letters for the class, identity code, number of persons, weight restrictions and type of aircraft. Also listed are the colours of signal flares for airfield traffic control.

Einteilung der Flugzeuge / Signale / Hoheitszeichen

a) Einteilung der Flugzeuge in Deutschland

1. Nach der Zulassungsklasse

Klasse	Zeichen	Personen	Fluggewicht
A—1	D—Y . . .	1—2	bis 500 kg
A—2	D—E . . .	1—3	„ 1000 kg
B—1	D—I . . .	1—3	„ 2500 kg
B—2	D—O . . .	4—6	„ 2500 kg
C—1	D—U . . .	über 6	über 2500 kg
C—2	D—A . . .	„ 6	„ 2500 kg

Flugzeuge der Luftwaffe WL — statt D—.

2. Nach der Verwendungsgruppe

H = Höchstleistungsflugzeuge
G = Güterflugzeuge
P = Personenflugzeuge (gewerbsmäßig)
R = Reiseflugzeuge (privat)
S = Schulflugzeuge (nur Klasse A—2)
K = Kunstflugzeuge.

3. Nach der Beanspruchungsgruppe

1 sehr gering
2 gering
3 normal
4 hoch
5 sehr hoch

Beispiel: Ein Flugzeug der Klasse B—2 (Bezeichnung D—OVIP) ist zugelassen für G 4 und P 3, das heißt für Güterbeförderung mit hoher oder Personenbeförderung im Verkehr mit normaler Beanspruchung.

b) Signale und Zeichen im Flugbetrieb

Eine rote Leuchtkugel: Gefahr, Landebahn nicht frei.
Drei rote Leuchtkugeln: Höchste Gefahr. Nur im äußersten Notfall landen.
Drei Rauchpatronen (tags): Landeaufforderung.
Drei grüne Leuchtsterne (nachts): Landeaufforderung.
Eine weiße Leuchtkugel: Hebt die vorherigen Zeichen auf. — Landebahn ist frei. — Nachts: Hier ist der Platz!
Roter Ball am Signalmast: Startverbot.

3. Other Markings

An identification plate giving name and address of manufacturer, aircraft type, construction number, year of manufacture of each part is to be firmly affixed to the fuselage, wings and other parts of the aircraft.

On the left rear fuselage, in black characters of at least 25 mm height and 4 mm thickness on light background, the following information must be stencilled:

a) name and address of owner
b) tare weight, payload and maximum take-off weight in kg.
c) maximum number of persons, including crew.
d) date of last annual inspection and due date of next inspection.

Airships carry this information in a prominent place on the gondola. In the cargo hold, a diagram showing stowing of cargo is to be affixed.

On **engines**, a metal plate with the following details has to be affixed in a prominent place:

a) name and address of manufacturer
b) type, series, construction number and year
c) maximum power and maximum permissible RPM

In case where **advertising** is to be applied, the following exceptions are permitted :

For **biplanes**, advertising lettering to be applied as follows:

National letter **"D"** and registration	Advertising
Top surfaces of upper wing (standard size)	Under lower wing
Undersides of fuselage (standard size)	
Rear third of fuselage sides (as large and obvious as possible)	Forward third of fuselage sides

On **monoplanes**:

National letter **"D"** and registration	Advertising
Top surfaces of wing (standard size)	Underside of wing
Underside of fuselage (standard size)	
Rear third of fuselage sides (as large as possible)	
Uderside of tailplane and elevator (as large as possible)	Forward two-thirds of fuselage sides

Should more than one aircraft carry the same advertising, prominent distinguishing marks, e.g. identification numbers (*TRUMF I, II* etc.), should be shown if possible.

No advertising is permitted on aircraft on scheduled services!

Advertising aircraft can only be operated within germany, applications for exceptions to be submitted the the *Reich* Air ministry through local air offices (*Luftamter*).

Aircraft and **airships** undergoing flight tests with **blind flying equipment** or autopilot carry an identification mark consisting of two light yellow bands around the fuselage.

The use of **red** on aircraft is prohibited (except for the national flag on the fin).

Berlin, 29 August 1936 - Reichsgesetzblatt No. 78
Publication of amended version of air traffic regulations of 21 August 1936.

ABOVE: The rear fuselage of Henschel Hs 123V1/U1 D-ILUA showing the position of the standard stencilling. However it would appear that not all the weight information has been provided.

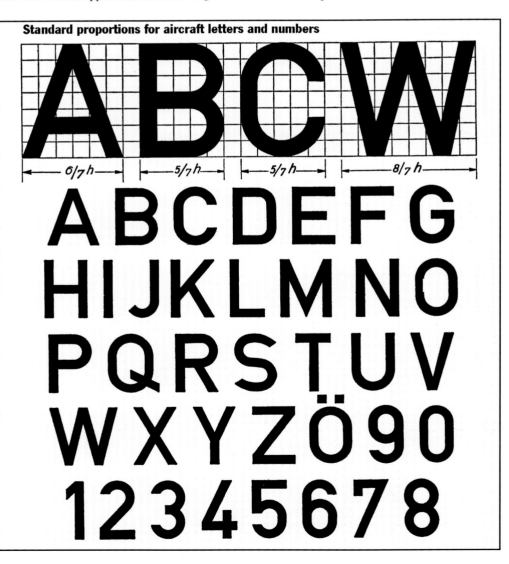

Standard proportions for aircraft letters and numbers

BELOW: These He 51 A-1s which have just been delivered to Reklamestaffel Mitteldeutschland carry civil registrations. The unit was to retain these until the Luftwaffe was publicly revealed to the world in March 1935, after which time the five character code system was adopted. By September 1936 however, this too had been replaced by a system of coloured numbers and symbols.

ABOVE: Adolf Galland seen here in France in 1940 shortly after taking command of III./JG 26. Galland was amongst those German trainee pilots to receive fighter training in Italy during 1933. Galland described the facilities in Italy as "grossly inadequate".

"Our Jagdgeschwader was an elite unit"

GEORG KEIL

BELOW: A group of Luftwaffe pilots of the Reklamestaffel Mitteldeutschland debriefing in Döberitz in 1935

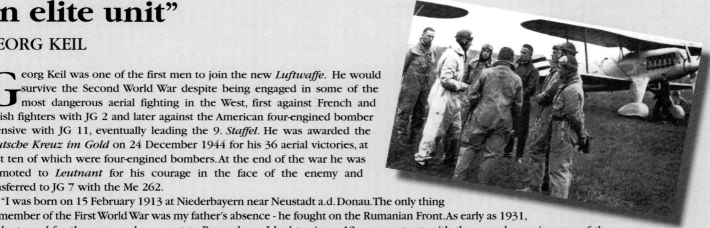

Georg Keil was one of the first men to join the new *Luftwaffe*. He would survive the Second World War despite being engaged in some of the most dangerous aerial fighting in the West, first against French and British fighters with JG 2 and later against the American four-engined bomber offensive with JG 11, eventually leading the 9. *Staffel*. He was awarded the *Deutsche Kreuz im Gold* on 24 December 1944 for his 36 aerial victories, at least ten of which were four-engined bombers. At the end of the war he was promoted to *Leutnant* for his courage in the face of the enemy and transferred to JG 7 with the Me 262.

"I was born on 15 February 1913 at Niederbayern near Neustadt a.d. Donau. The only thing I remember of the First World War was my father's absence - he fought on the Rumanian Front. As early as 1931, I volunteered for the army and was sent to Regensburg. I had to sign a 12 year contract with the army, becoming one of the 100,000 men officially allowed by the Treaty of Versailles. I then underwent a series of technical courses to become a mechanic. Having success with these I was chosen, with a number of comrades, to serve with the *Reklamestaffel Mitteldeutschland* at Berlin-Döberitz. In fact its name (translated as "Publicity Squadron") was merely a screen to hide a unit with a totally military structure and goal. I don't remember our aircraft ever being painted with publicity messages to show them over Berlin or its suburbs. A second *Gruppe* was added to the unit at Jüterbog in April 1935.

"The first aircraft type that we had at Döberitz was the Arado 64, followed by the Ar 65 and He 51. In 1935 I decided to apply to become a pilot and was sent to Schleissheim near München. After training for a year I returned to the same unit at Döberitz which had now been redesignated JG 132 *"Richthofen"*. Our *Kommodore* was *Obstlt.* Gerd von Massow.

"I again served with the I. *Gruppe* under *Major* Carl Viek. Our *Kapitän* (of the 2. *Staffel*) was *Hptm.* Hans-Hugo Witt (later *Kommodore* of JG 26) but he was soon replaced by *Oblt.* Erich Bode (later *Kommandeur* of II./JG 26) and finally *Oblt.* von Blomberg, the son of the Minister of Defence.

"I was then short-listed to go to Spain but, because I was married, I was not selected. Now (and then too) I consider that our *Jagdgeschwader* was an elite unit: we were taught by very experienced pilots, several of whom had served in the First World War. War experience is invaluable in a military unit. In addition, some of our pilots had undergone the very rare experience of being trained in Russia. In fact in the late 1920s and early 1930s no-one, except those who had been trained in Russia or Italy, could match their abilities.

"We participated from a distance in the operation against Czechoslovakia in 1938, being put on alert at Döberitz, but did not have to intervene. Our main task was to prevent the Berlin area from being bombed but, of course, that never happened."

ABOVE: Taken inside a hangar, probably at Jever on the North Sea coast, this photo shows a group of He 51s of 1./Küstenfliegergruppe 136. In conformity with the policy of the time, the aircraft have their five character codes repeated on the top of the wing, "60" on the port wing, inboard of the Balkenkreuz, the individual letter in centre and the Staffel and Gruppe number "41" on the starboard wing.

BELOW: The most successful and famous German fighter pilot of the First World War, Manfred Freiherr von Richthofen (left) shakes hands with the Commander-in-Chief of the Luftstreitkräfte (German Army Air Service), Generalleutnant von Hoeppner. Von Richthofen was to record 80 aerial victories before he was killed on 21 April 1918. The exact circumstances of his death still remain unproven. On 14 March 1935, in the presence of Hitler, I./JG 132 was named "Richthofen" in honour of von Richthofen, the "Red Baron".

LEFT: Robert von Greim was born in 1892, joining the Bavarian Army in 1911. In 1916 he transferred to the Flying Service, rising to command first Jasta 34 and then Jagdgruppe 10. By the end of the war he had 26 victories and had been awarded the Pour le Mérite on 10 October 1918. After assisting Chiang Kai-shek organise an air force in China, he returned to Germany and formed the DVS at Berlin-Staaken. While serving there he established Reklamestaffel Mitteldeutschland which became the Luftwaffe's first fighter Gruppe. He led this unit until he became Inspector of Fighters and Dive Bombers in April 1935. In 1936 he was made Inspector of Equipment and Flight Safety and next year became Luftwaffe Head of Personnel. Towards the end of April 1945 Hitler appointed him to replace Göring as Commander-in-Chief of the Luftwaffe but von Griem committed suicide shortly before being taken prisoner. Here Generalmajor von Greim wears full Luftwaffe dress uniform with the Pour le Mérite at his neck.

Luftkreiskommando areas 1 April 1934

	Luftkreiskommando 1	Königsberg
	Luftkreiskommando 2	Berlin
	Luftkreiskommando 3	Dresden
	Luftkreiskommando 4	Münster
	Luftkreiskommando 5	München
	Luftkreiskommando 6	Kiel (Naval Units)*
	* Naval units had no designated area	

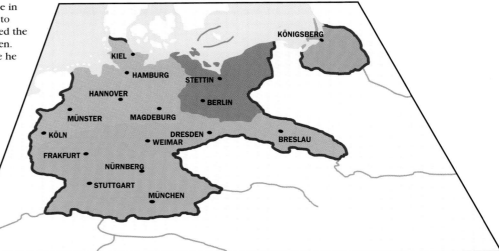

ABOVE: A Kette (flight of three) He 51 A-1s from I./JG 132 taxying prior to taking off. The aircraft carry the "Traditional Colour" red engine cowlings but, at this stage, this was not extended to the upper fuselage decking.

ABOVE: Late in 1935 the old system of using civil registrations to identify Luftwaffe aircraft was abandoned in favour of a five character code. This comprised two numbers, a letter and two further numbers. The sequence was painted on both sides of the fuselage, and repeated above and below the wings. When applied to the wings, the first two figures were painted on the port side of the top wing, the second two on the starboard side, all inboard of the Balkenkreuz. The individual letter was sometimes painted on the top of the fuselage, on the centre of the wing, or omitted altogether. This photo shows a He 51 21+L11 of 1./JG 132 with several Ju 52/3ms in the background.

Assignment of "Traditional Military Colours"

A directive from the Oberbefehlshabers der Luftwaffe (LA Nr. 1290/36 geh. LA II/Fl. In. 3) dated 2 July 1936, gave detailed descriptions regarding markings for fighter aircraft to which all units had to comply by the 1 September 1936. Because the five figure code system was open to confusion the introduction of "Traditional Colours" were bestowed on several Geschwadern which were initially applied to the nose and later extended to the upper fuselage decking.

JG 131	black	(Jesau)
JG 132 "Richthofen"	red	(Döberitz)
JG 134 "Horst Wessel"	brown	(Dortmund)
JG 232	green	(Bernburg)
JG 233	blue	(Bad Aibling)
JG 234	orange	(Köln)

LEFT AND ABOVE: A formation of He 51s, painted pale grey overall, belonging to the 1. Staffel/Jagdgeschwader 132 "Richthofen" fly over another two aircraft. The unit had adopted the five character code system and also the new "Traditional Colour" red on the fuselage noses. Taking the aircraft in the foreground, 21+D11, the code could be broken down as follows:

2 Luftkreiskommando II
1 The first Geschwader formed within that Luftkreis (in this case JG 132)
D The individual aircraft identification letter
1 The I. Gruppe
1 The 1. Staffel

LEFT AND BELOW: As far as is known, only three Luftwaffe fighter units, JG 132, JG 135 and JG 136, definitely carried the five character code which replaced civil markings for military aircraft in 1935. The first two numbers of the code, in this case "21", indicated the first Geschwader formed within Luftkreiskommando II, e.g. JG 132. The letter was the individual aircraft, the third number indicated the Gruppe to which the aircraft belonged, e.g. I./JG 132, and the final number the Staffel, in this case 1./JG 132. What remains a mystery is why I./JG 135, which was not formed until March 1937, by which time the colourful markings stipulated in Directive LA Nr. 1290/36 geh LAQ II/FI dated 2 July 1936 were adopted, carried this form of marking.

Earliest style black and white Balkenkreuz

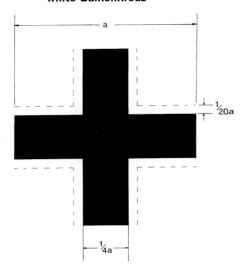

Heinkel He 51 A-1
An aircraft of the Aerobatic Staffel (2./JG 132 "Richthofen") at Berlin-Staaken, 22 March 1936. This aircraft carries the typical five character code system adopted by all Luftwaffe units around October 1935. The code was also painted on top of the upper wing and below the lower wing. At this time, the starboard side of the rudder would be painted in black, white and red horizontal stripes with black uppermost.

ABOVE AND COLOUR PROFILE: This He 51 was photographed at Berlin-Staaken on Luftwaffe Day, 22 March 1936. It belonged to the 2. Staffel of JG 132 "Richthofen".

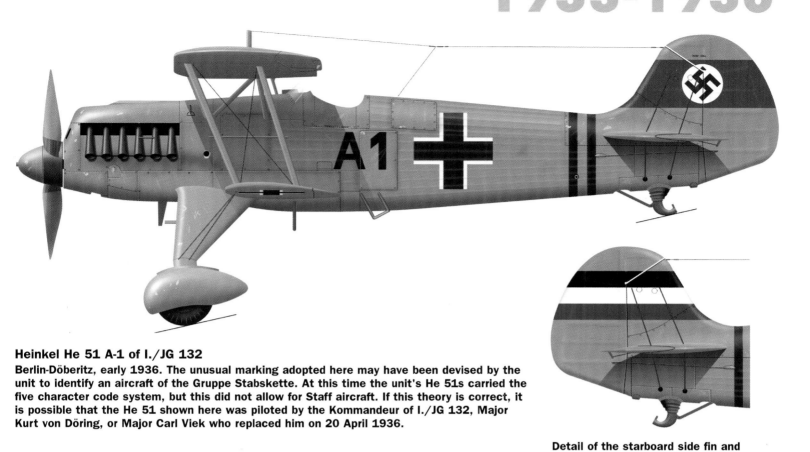

Heinkel He 51 A-1 of I./JG 132

Berlin-Döberitz, early 1936. The unusual marking adopted here may have been devised by the unit to identify an aircraft of the Gruppe Stabskette. At this time the unit's He 51s carried the five character code system, but this did not allow for Staff aircraft. If this theory is correct, it is possible that the He 51 shown here was piloted by the Kommandeur of I./JG 132, Major Kurt von Döring, or Major Carl Viek who replaced him on 20 April 1936.

Detail of the starboard side fin and rudder markings. This was introduced in 1935 but was replaced in the middle of 1936 by the red horizontal band and Hakenkreuz inside a white circle.

LEFT AND ABOVE: These two photos show a He 51 A-1 with the unusual marking "A1" and two black rear fuselage bands. Belonging to a part of I./JG 132 (Jagdgruppe Döberitz) the marking may have been used by the Kommandeur of the Gruppe, Major Kurt von Döring (or Major Carl Viek who replaced him on 20 April 1936). At this time the aircraft of JG 132 carried the five character code system, but as there was no obvious marking for the Stabskette, the unit may have adopted the variation shown here.

LEFT: A Staffel of Ar 65 F fighters in formation. Note that the aircraft are flying in groups of three, the so-called Kette element, a formation adopted by most countries between the wars. Operations by J 88 in the Spanish Civil War were to prove that this grouping was flawed in combat because one aircraft could cover another, but the third machine would be unprotected. The new formation of two aircraft, the Rotte, was adopted at the instigation of Oblt. Werner Mölders who led 3./J 88 in Spain.

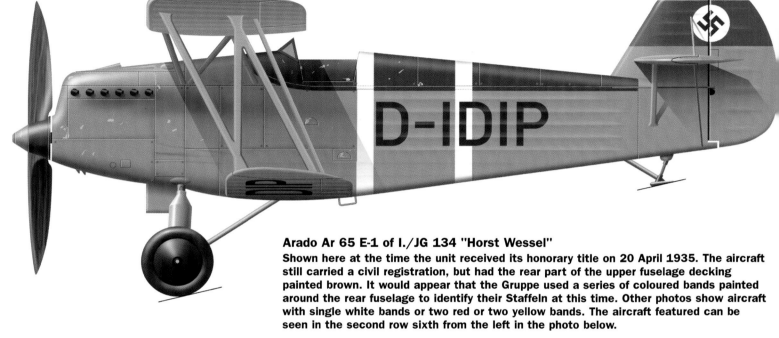

Arado Ar 65 E-1 of I./JG 134 "Horst Wessel"
Shown here at the time the unit received its honorary title on 20 April 1935. The aircraft still carried a civil registration, but had the rear part of the upper fuselage decking painted brown. It would appear that the Gruppe used a series of coloured bands painted around the rear fuselage to identify their Staffeln at this time. Other photos show aircraft with single white bands or two red or two yellow bands. The aircraft featured can be seen in the second row sixth from the left in the photo below.

RIGHT: An aerial photograph taken on 20 April 1935, during the ceremony at which JG 134 received its honorary title "Horst Wessel". Assembled in three neat rows are some of the unit's He 51 and Ar 65 single-engined fighters, with the He 51s to the left. At this time, JG 134's Heinkels were left in natural metal finish but their Ar 65s were painted pale grey. Both still carried civil registrations. To the left of the picture, at the top, can be seen Hitler's personal Ju 52/3m registered D-2600.

LEFT: As the clandestine Luftwaffe developed, other more radical and innovative aircarft were being developed in Germany such as the Bf 109. The V 1 Prototype seen here made its first flight at Augsburg on 28 May 1935 piloted by the Messerschmitt test pilot Hans-Dietrich Knoetzsch. The aircraft was powered by a 695 hp Rolls-Royce Kestrel engine.

LEFT: A Kette He 51s from JG 134 "Horst Wessel" fly over Nürnberg Zeppelinfeld during a Nazi Party rally. The name was to remain with the unit following its progressive redesignation as JG 142, ZG 26 and JG 6.

BELOW Hitler (centre) having arrived for the JG 134 naming ceremony talks to an unidentified Party official.

BELOW: Hitler and Göring (second and third from the left) with a crowd of officials from the Luftwaffe and the Nazi Party examine one of JG 134's He 51s on 20 April 1935. At this time the unit comprised two Gruppen: I./JG 134 which was commanded by Major Josef Kammhuber and II./JG 134 by Major Theo Osterkamp. Kammhuber was later to command the German night fighter force.

BELOW RIGHT: Hitler inspects one of JG 134's Heinkel 51s during the ceremony at which the unit received its honorary title of "Horst Wessel". At this time, April 1935, the aircraft still carried German civil registrations and the "Traditional Colour", in this case brown, had yet to be applied. At Hitler's side is Stabschef 1. Adjutant, Oberführer Riemann.

ABOVE: A group of "schwarze Männer" ("black men" or mechanics) pose around a He 51, "White 12" of 3./JG 132.

ABOVE: Unfortunately the first two figures of the code on this group of He 51s cannot be seen on this photo, but the aircraft are thought to have been operated by II./JG 132. Note that the He 51 in the foreground has the name "Jaguar" painted above the undercarriage fairing, and the second the name "Panther".

RIGHT: During the pre-war period a large number of propaganda photos of Luftwaffe fighters were taken, most showing their aircraft arranged in neat rows. This photo shows 3./JG 132 at Döberitz near Berlin.

Staffeln and Gruppen markings - 1936	
1., 4., and 7. Staffel	no marking
2., 5., and 8. Staffel	white band
3., 6., and 9. Staffel	white circle
Staffel leader normally flew Number "1" aircraft with no additional markings.	
Gruppen within Geschwader markings	
I. Gruppe	no markings
II. Gruppe	horizontal white bar
III. Gruppe	horizontal white wavy line

"Our best fighter of the time..."

HENNIG STRÜMPELL

"In 1931 I joined my Grandfather's regiment as an 18 year old *Fahnenjunker* (cadet) and quickly volunteered to become a pilot. It was a goal that I had not much chance of attaining: the Treaty of Versailles having forbidden Germany to have an air force. We knew, however, that a *Luftwaffe* had been created secretly. In spite of some eye problems (that I could more or less hide), I was accepted in the DLV (*Deutsche Luftsportverband*) at Cottbus. It was here that I met the great Udet, an ace of the First World War. I learned to fly in an aircraft which his company had produced. I flew the Heinkel *Kadett*, the Focke-Wulf *Stieglitz* and Junkers W 34. My unit was not political but we still regarded Hitler with some hope: he was the only man who could save Germany from her miserable situation. But, we were very suspicious of the troops of the S.A.

"After I asked to become a fighter pilot, I was posted to Schleissheim where I met several Generals such as von Schleich and Milch. I received excellent instruction on such types as the *Stösser* at Fassberg, and finished on our first fighter aircraft, the He 51, again at Schleissheim. My training as a fighter pilot came to an end in 1934, at the same time as the new *Luftwaffe* was officially formed. In April 1936 I was posted, naturally, to a fighter squadron under formation. This was I./JG 232 which was being established first at Döberitz and later Bernburg, from elements provided by the famous JG 132 *"Richthofen"*. My *Staffelkapitän* was *Hptm*. Hannes Gentzen, who would become the first official ace of the World War Two with seven aircraft shot down during the Polish campaign. On 23 April 1936, I flew the Arado 76 for the first time and on the same day, I began to training on our best fighter of the time, the Heinkel 51. The Fw 56 quickly replaced the Ar 76 in the training units.

"On 1 September 1936, I was posted to the Legion Condor, where I remained until April 1937. When I came back, I went to 3./JG 132 at Berlin/Döberitz where I became adjutant to the famous Bruno Loerzer, a World War One ace who had been awarded the *Pour le Mérite* like his comrade Göring. At that time, the fighter squadrons in Germany were also being equipped with the Messerschmitt 109, although several He 51s were still in service. At the end of 1937, the latter completely disappeared from the front-line units. Loerzer and I expanded the *Gruppe*, receiving many additional pilots including Galland, Hrabak and Brustellin who were later to become famous in World War Two. On 1st November 1938, our I./JG 132 was renamed I./JG 131."

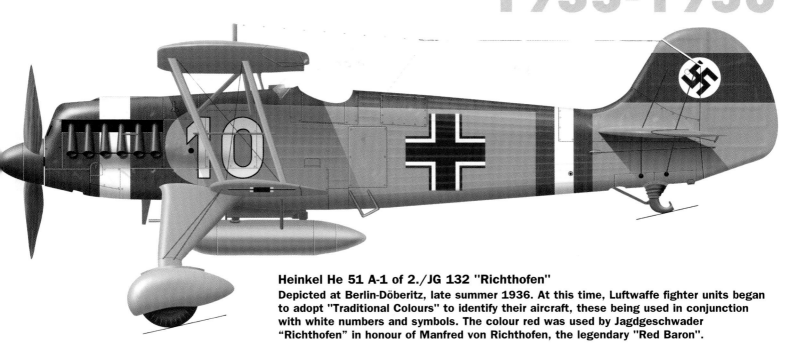

Heinkel He 51 A-1 of 2./JG 132 "Richthofen"
Depicted at Berlin-Döberitz, late summer 1936. At this time, Luftwaffe fighter units began to adopt "Traditional Colours" to identify their aircraft, these being used in conjunction with white numbers and symbols. The colour red was used by Jagdgeschwader "Richthofen" in honour of Manfred von Richthofen, the legendary "Red Baron".

ABOVE: The American aviator, Charles Lindbergh (third from the left) watches as machine-gun calibration tests are carried out on a He 51 A-1 of 2./JG 132 during a visit he paid to the unit at Berlin-Döberitz during the summer of 1936. Lindbergh became famous after completing the first solo flight of the Atlantic Ocean on 21 May 1927 in his "Spirit of St.Louis". From 1935 he moved to Europe, making tours of several countries. In 1938 he was to receive a decoration from Hitler and praised the Luftwaffe as "superior to that of any other European country."

ABOVE: This group of nine He 51s was photographed flying over the Rhine near Köln in March 1936 at the time of the re-occupation of the Rhineland. The six aircraft in the foreground are 21+C22, 21+E23, 21+E21 and 21+F21 from II./JG 132 and 23+Z11 and 23+Y12 from the dive bomber unit I./St.G 162. The three He 51s in the background appear to have white numbers aft of the fuselage crosses and possibly belonged to III./JG 134. This marking scheme was probably adopted as an interim measure for the Rhineland operation.

LEFT: The Ar 68 was the second aircraft designed by Dipl.-Ing. Walter Blume after he took over from Rethel as chief designer at Arado. Initially, service pilots expressed some misgivings as to whether the Ar 68 had any advantages over the He 51, but a mock battle staged between the two by Ernst Udet quickly proved the Arado superior on all counts. It soon became a familiar sight on Luftwaffe airfields during the middle 1930s and soldiered on as a trainer until the end of the war.

RIGHT: A line-up of Ar 68 Es of Jagdgeschwader 134 "Horst Wessel". On 7 March 1936 Germany re-occupied the Rhineland which had been declared a demilitarised zone by the Versailles Treaty. The occupying troops were supported by the He 51s of II./JG 132, the Ar 68s of III./JG 134 and the He 51s from I./St.G 162 "Immelmann". After circling Köln cathedral at midday, several Ar 68s and He 51s landed at the city's Butzweilerhof airfield. Hannes Trautloft, who was serving with III./JG 134 at the time, described the operation as "… a great moment". Following their arrival at Köln the unit was to fly several exercises and manouvres. The aircraft shown here carry the markings adopted for one of these exercises.

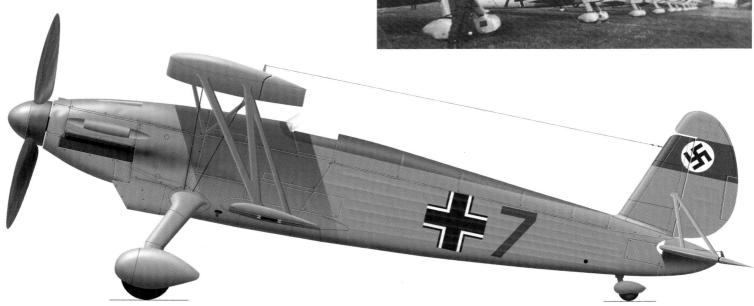

Arado Ar 68 E-1 of III./JG 134 "Horst Wessel"
Depicted here at Köln-Butzweilerhof, March 1936. Following the re-occupation of the Rhineland in March 1936, aircraft of III./JG 134 flew a series of demonstration flights around the area. For this, their aircraft were marked with red numbers positioned behind the fuselage Balkenkreuz.

LEFT AND ABOVE: The Ar 68 progressively replaced the Ar 65 in Luftwaffe service. Two main versions were built, the Ar 68 E powered by the 680 hp Jumo 210 D engine and the Ar 68 F with the 750 hp BMW VI 7,3Z engine. Relatively few of the former were delivered because of production problems with the Jumo power plant. Here an Ar 68 E-1, "Red 8", is shown flying over the Köln area during exercises.

BELOW: A line-up of Ar 68 Fs of III./JG 134 at Köln-Butzweilerhof in March 1936. These aircraft, which took part in the demonstration flights preceding the re-occupation of the Rhineland, carry an individual number aft of the Balkenkreuz.

RIGHT AND BELOW: Following the re-occupation of the Rhineland on 7 March 1936, the Ar 68 Fs of 8. and 9./JG 134 flew a number of demonstration flights over the area to dissuade France and Britain from intervening. Shortly afterwards, the unit formed the basis of I./JG 234 at Köln under Hptm. Walter Grabmann.

BELOW: This Focke-Wulf 44 was operated by JG 134 "Horst Wessel" as interim equipment before the unit received its first He 51s. Note the Focke-Wulf insignia above the undercarriage. The Fw 44 *Stieglitz* (Goldfinch) first flew in the summer of 1932 but displayed many faults. Exhaustive testing by Kurt Tank led to considerable redesign until the aircraft emerged as a trainer with excellent flying characteristics. The first major production model was the Fw 44 C, seen here, was powered by a 150 hp Siemens Sh 14 A radial engine.

BELOW: Another photo of the colours being presented to I./JG 134 on 15 May 1936 with Ernst Udet on the left. The designation "JG 134" indicated the unit's position within its allocated Luftkreis; the second digit "3" signifying the type of unit it was, in this case "3" = fighters; the third digit "4" was the number of the Luftkreis, in this case Luftkreis IV in Münster.

BELOW: The Nazi hierarchy attached great importance to tradition. Here, General der Flieger Erhard Milch presents the unit colour to an officer of I./Jagdgeschwader 134 at Dortmund on 15 May 1936. The officer may have been the unit Kommandeur, Major Josef Kammhuber who later became the head of the German night fighter force. The Geschwader had been named "Horst Wessel" on 20 April 1935 in remembrance of the young Berlin SA leader who was murdered in a street brawl with some Communists in February 1930.

Arado Ar 68 F-1 of 4./JG 134 "Horst Wessel"
Depicted at Werl near Dortmund, 1937, this aircraft had a white number "11" painted on either side and beneath the fuselage as well as above the centre section of the upper wing, all outlined in black. The similarly painted horizontal bar identified the second Gruppe. JG 134's "Traditional Colour" brown was often edged with a thin line of the same colour.

ABOVE: A group of mechanics pose in front of an Ar 68 F of Jagdgeschwader "Horst Wessel". The aircraft has the engine cowling and upper fuselage decking painted in the Geschwader colour brown. From 1 September 1936 German fighters began to adopt these colours which, by April of the following year, comprised black for JG 131, red for JG 132, brown for JG 134, blue for JG 135, green for JG 232 (later JG 137) and orange for JG 234.

LEFT: These two Ar 68 Fs were flown by 4./JG 134 "Horst Wessel" which was based at Werl. The brown engine cowling and upper fuselage decking is unusual in that it is edged with a thin brown line, a not uncommon practice with JG 134. The white horizontal bar beneath the cockpit edged in black indicated that the aircraft was operated by the second Gruppe.

RIGHT: During the autumn of 1936, the cowlings and upper fuselage decking of the "Horst Wessel" Geschwader's aircraft were painted brown - to match the uniform shirt colour worn by the Nazi Party at this time. This photo shows a line-up of Ar 68 Fs, probably from the 1. Staffel (no band or circle on the nose or on the rear fuselage band) of the I. Gruppe (no horizontal bar or wavy line in front of the Balkenkreuz).

LEFT: The fuselage of this Ar 68 E-1 of 6./JG 134 has been loaded on to a lorry for transport to a repair depot. The aircraft has a white horizontal bar positioned forward of the fuselage Balkenkreuz which indicated that it was operated by the second Gruppe. The white circle indicated the third Staffel in that Gruppe, in other words 6./JG 134.

RIGHT: An interesting photo of an Ar 68 F-1 with coloured engine cowling and upper fuselage decking, obviously taken before the remainder of its markings were applied. The aircraft possibly belonged to II./JG 134 which was unusual in having a thin brown outline added to its brown Geschwader colour.

ABOVE: Photographed at Dedelsdorf, this He 51 carries the double chevron and vertical bar indicating that it was piloted by the Gruppenkommandeur of the second Gruppe of a Luftwaffe fighter unit. The unit was probably II./JG 134 which, at this time, was commanded by Major Theodor Osterkamp.

ABOVE: This photo of a He 51 still in standard 1935 markings, which was dropped in the middle of 1936, is of particular interest as it shows the tail wheel towing device that allowed ground crews to manoeuver aircraft around the airfield.

Heinkel He 51 A-1 of Stab II./JG 134 "Horst Wessel"
At Dedelsdorf, 1937, JG 134 adopted the "Traditional Colour" brown because of its connection with one of the most notorious "Brown Shirts", Horst Wessel. The Gruppenkommandeur's aircraft, shown here, was identified by the double chevron, this marking being used right up to the end of the Second World War. At this time the commander of II./JG 134 was Major Theodor Osterkamp.

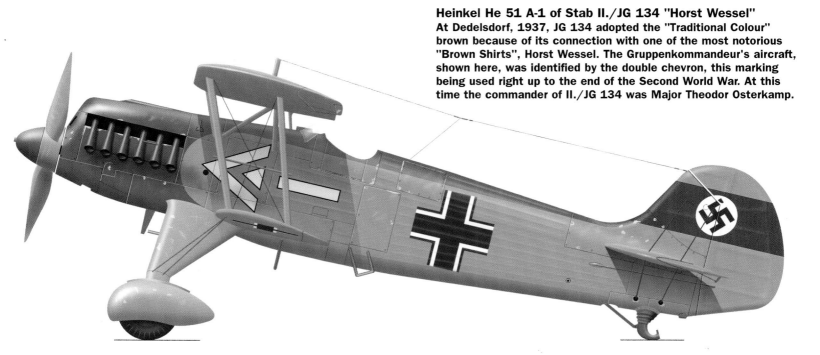

RIGHT: This He 51 B-2 of 2./Küstenjagdgruppe 136 carries the five character code system. The first pair of numbers (e.g. "60") indicated an autonomous Gruppe within Luftkreiskommando 6, the third number (e.g. "4") the fourth autonomous Gruppe formed within that Luftkreiskommando and the last number (e.g. "2") was the Staffel to which the aircraft belonged.

BELOW: The prototype He 51 D floatplane which had twin bay wings. The aircraft is shown mounted on its twin-wheel ground handling dolly. A small number of Heinkel He 51 B-2 floatplanes were delivered to Küstenjagdgruppe 136 based near the old naval aviation barracks at Kiel-Holtenau on the North Sea coast.

BELOW A number of He 51 B-2 floatplanes were flown by I./JG 136. Although the unit's home base was Jever on the North Sea coast, these aircraft probably operated from Kiel-Holtenau which had the necessary harbour facilities. The addition of floats reduced the maximum speed of the He 51 from 330 km/h (205 mph) to 318 km/h (197 mph).

Heinkel He 51 B-2 floatplane of 1./Küstenjagdgruppe 136
Based at Kiel-Holtenau, late 1936, 1./Kü.J.Gr 136, like all other Luftwaffe fighter units, adopted the new system of markings which were introduced by September 1936. Unlike most Jagdgruppen, however, Kü.J.Gr 136 (later I./JG 136) did not use a "Traditional Colour" painted on its engine cowlings and upper fuselage decking.

ABOVE, LEFT AND BELOW: Several He 51 B-2 floatplanes were delivered to 1./Küstenjagdgruppe 136 at Kiel-Holtenau for coastal defence. The unit, which was later redesignated I./JG 136, did not have the engine cowlings and upper fuselage decking of its aircraft painted in a "Traditional Colour" as did most of the other Luftwaffe fighter units of the time. The aircraft was painted pale grey (63) overall with the exception of the floats which were finished in natural metal. A special black anti-fouling compound, known as Avionorm Bitumenlack 120, was usually added to the underwater sections finishing at the high water mark on the upper surfaces of each float.

LEFT: Luftwaffe ground crews look on as the twin 7.9 mm machine guns of this He 51 B-2 floatplane are calibrated with the aid of a white disc which temporarily replaced the propeller.

ABOVE: The port undercarriage leg of this He 51 collapsed on landing at Jever airfield. The aircraft, which was operated by 1./Kü.J.Gr 136, carries its five character code 60+A41 painted in black on both sides of the fuselage, on top of the upper wing and beneath the lower wing.

ABOVE: Unlike most of the other early Luftwaffe fighter units, Küstenjagdstaffel 136, which later became I./JG 136, never carried "Traditional Colour" markings on the nose and upperfuselage decking of their aircraft. The first two He 51 A-1s in this picture, which still carry the five character codes 60+L41 and 60+D41 were operated by 1./Kü.J.Gr 136.

RIGHT: He 51 A-1s of 1./Küstenjagdstaffel 136 at Jever in early 1936, make final preparations for a flight.

Heinkel He 51 A-1 of 1./Küstenjagdstaffel 136
At Jever, early 1936, this unit, like Jagdgeschwader 132, carried the five character code system. In this case, the first pair of numbers, "60", indicated an autonomous Gruppe within Luftkreis-kommando 6, the third number, "4", the fourth autonomous Gruppe formed within that Luftkreiskommando and the last number, "1", was the Staffel to which the aircraft belonged. The letter "E" was the aircraft's individual identification.

LEFT: This photo is somewhat of a mystery! The double chevron markings of a Gruppenkommandeur have been painted on the fuselage sides of this He 51 A, but the aircraft also carries the five character code system.

BELOW: Many of the early Luftwaffe fighter units were initially equipped with trainers such as the He 72. These aircraft, neatly parked in a large hangar at Bernburg, belong to I./JG 232 which was formed on 1 April 1936. Also known as "Gruppe Loerzer" and "Jagdverband Bernburg" the unit was redesignated I./JG 137 later in the year. This Gruppe eventually formed the basis of I.(Jagd)/LG 2 and I./ZG 2.

BELOW: I./JG 136 grew out of Fliegerstaffel (J) 1 at Kiel-Holtenau for the task of coastal defence. The unit was initially equipped with a mixture of Arado 64s and 65s and Heinkel HD 38s and He 51s. The two latter types were sometimes fitted with floats and were designed to be catapult launched. In this photo are, seated - left to right, Uffz. Fritz Schwering, Uffz. Helmut Goedert and Ofw. Gerhard Kadow with Ofw. Richard Brunner, Ofw. Fritz Kube and Ofw. Hermann Roth lying in front.

BELOW: A group of He 51s all carrying the code "60", an individual letter and "42" on their fuselage sides. The first pair of numbers indicated an autonomous Gruppe within Luftkreiskommando 6, the third number (e.g. "4") the fourth autonomous Gruppe formed within that Luftkreiskommando (in this case Küstenjagdgruppe 136) and the last number (e.g. "2") was the Staffel to which the aircraft belonged.

BELOW: I./JG 232 was created at Bernburg on 1 April 1936 from a nucleus provided by II./JG 132, receiving the He 51 single-engined fighter as its initial equipment. D-IPTI, the victim of the soft ground at Bernburg, is seen performing what Luftwaffe slang referred to as a "Fliegerdenkmal" ("Monument to the Aviator"). Note that the wheel spats have been removed to ease maintenance.

ABOVE: Another two-seat primary trainer used in large numbers by the Luftwaffe was the Arado Ar 66. Designed by Dipl.-Ing. Walter Rethel, over 10,000 aircraft were built. The production version, the Ar 66 C, was powered by a 240 hp Argus As 10 C engine which gave it a maximum speed of 210 km/h (130 mph) at sea level. This aircraft, D-IVEX, suffered a minor mishap during the spring of 1936 while being piloted by a member of I./JG 232 at Bernburg.

LEFT: The two biplane trainers most used by the Luftwaffe's A/B Flugzeugführerschulen (primary training schools) were the Fw 44 and He 72. The aircraft to the left is a He 72 *Kadett* (Cadet) with a Fw 44 *Stieglitz* (Goldfinch) behind. The second letter "E" in the latter's civil registration indicates that it was in Class A2 and had an all-up weight of below 1,000 kg (2,200 lbs).

BELOW: The He 51 B-1 seen here differed from the A-1 in having increased undercarriage bracing and provision for a 170 litre (37.5 Imp gal) drop tank. The He 51 C-1, was a ground attack variant with provision for six 10 kg (22 lb) bombs beneath the wings and the C-2 had improved radio equipment. This variant was developed for use in Spain. Two other versions were proposed, the He 51 D and E, fitted with extended two-bay wings for high altitude operation but only a prototype of the former, with twin floats, was completed.

BELOW: A formation of eight He 51s from 3./JG 232 in flight near Bernburg, all fitted with auxiliary fuel tanks. The unit was later to be redesignated I./JG 137 with the re-organisation of the Luftkreiskommando as explained on page 50.

ABOVE: "White 3" of 2./JG 232 taxies along a snow covered runway at Bernburg during the winter of 1936-37. The He 51 carries the stripe band around its red painted cowling which identifies it as an aircraft of the second Staffel. This stripe was also painted around the rear fuselage, superimposed on a red band.

LEFT: A line-up of He 51s of 3./JG 232 at Bernburg. This unit had green engine cowlings and fuselage decking with white individual numbers edged in black. A white disk was painted on the engine cowling and rear fuselage band to identify the 3. Staffel. This marking was often repeated twice on top of the fuselage decking, in line with that on the cowling and just forward of the fuselage Balkenkreuz.

RIGHT: On 2 July 1936 the Luftwaffe issued a directive which radically altered the markings applied to their fighters. From 1 September 1936 the aircraft were to adopt a system of colours, symbols and numbers. This line-up of the He 51s of 3./JG 232 shows the green engine cowling and fuselage decking adopted by this Geschwader, together with the white circle which identified the third Staffel within a Gruppe. The large white numbers painted in white edged in black identified the individual aircraft.

RIGHT: The Fw 56 *Stösser* was designed by Dipl.-Ing. Kurt Tank as a lightweight fighter and advanced trainer for the fledgling Luftwaffe. The prototype made its first flight in November 1933 powered by a 240 hp Argus As 10 C engine. The Fw 56 A-1 production model, an example of which is shown here, began to leave the assembly lines in 1935. This aircraft carries the German civilian all letter registration system introduced in April 1934. The first two letters of the code DINSA indicate Germany ("D" for Deutschland) and an aircraft with an all-up weight of below 1,000 kg (2,200 lbs) and one to three seats ("I"). The aircraft in the background are a Ju 52/3m (to the left) and a Fw 44.

A contemporary German watercolour painting depicting a typical scene of He 51 Jagdstaffel pilots being briefed prior to a flight.

1933-1936

Arado Ar 68 E-1

Flown by the second Stabskette pilot of III./JG 132 at Jüterbog-Damm, autumn 1938. On 1 November 1938, this unit was redesignated II./JG 141, becoming I./ZG 76 in May 1939. At this time, Ar 68s began to adopt the black-green and dark green camouflage introduced originally for the Bf 109. The "wavy line" aft of the small number "2" indicated an aircraft of the second Gruppe. This line was supposed to be 1,098 mm (43.23 ins) long.

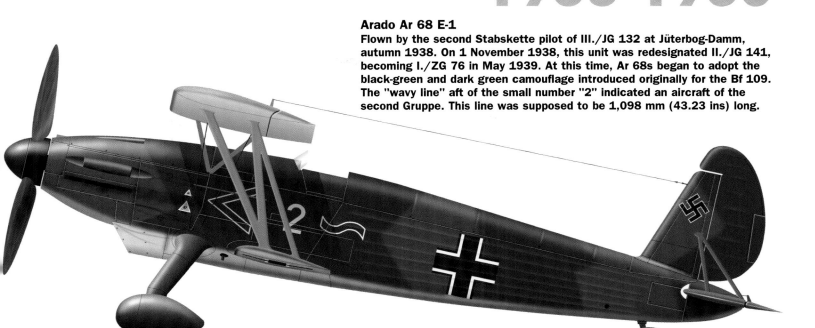

LEFT: The Ar 68 E in the foreground was flown by Lt. Helmut Riegel, Gruppenadjutant of III./JG 132. This unit was formed at Damm but moved to Fürstenwalde shortly afterwards where it was redesignated II./JG 141 in November 1938 and then I./ZG 76 in May 1939. Riegel's aircraft carries the single chevron which indicates the second aircraft in the Stabskette, this fact being emphasised by the white number "2". To contrast better with the dark green camouflage the wavy line, indicating the third Gruppe of a Geschwader, was painted black edged in white rather than the specified white.

BELOW: These Heinkel He 45 C-1 reconnaisance aircraft probably belonged to 3.(F)/122 based at Prenzlau. The colour photograph shows to advantage the pale grey finish which was carried by most Luftwaffe aircraft at the time.

REDESIGNATION OF LUFTWAFFE FIGHTER UNITS 1 MARCH 1935 TO 1 NOVEMBER 1938

1. I./JG 131 was formed at Jüterbog-Damm from a nucleus provided by II./JG 132, moving to Jesau shortly afterwards.

2. III./JG 132 was formed at Damm but moved to Furstenwalde shortly afterwards.

3. IV./JG 132 was formed from Jagdfliegerschule Werneuchen on 1 July 1938, moved to Oschatz shortly afterwards and, on 5 October 1938, to Karlsbad.

4. The exact date of the formation of I./JG 134 is unknown, although it did receive the honourary title of "Horst Wessel" on 20 April 1935.

5. II./JG 134 was formed from a basis provided by 5./JG 132 probably on 1 April 1936.

6. II.(schwere J)/LG was formed from a basis provided by the remains of III./JG 134, the 8. and 9. Staffeln of the unit forming I./JG 234.

7. IV./JG 134 was formed at Dortmund, moving first to Niesse and then to Lippstadt.

8. II./JG 135 moved shortly afterwards to Straubing and then to Herzogenaurach.

9. 1.Seejagdstaffel formed on 1 October 1934 from the Fliegerstaffel (J) at Kiel-Holtenau.

10. 4./JG 136 became 1.(leicht J)/LG shortly afterwards, 2. and 3.(leicht J)/LG being formed from 2. and 3./JG 137.

11. I./JG 232 was formed at Bernburg from a nucleus provided by JG 132, named "Gruppe Loerzer".

12. 2. and 3./JG 137 became 2. and 3.(leicht J)/LG at Garz on 1 February 1938. I./JG 137 had been made up to full strength again by 1 October 1938.

13. I./JG 234 was formed from 8. and 9./JG 134. The Geschwader was named "Schlageter" on 11 December 1938.

14. II./JG 234 was formed from a basis provided by 5./JG 134.

15. III./JG 234 was formed at Düsseldorf, moving first to Schweidnitz and then to Illesheim.

16. III./JG 334 originally proposed to be formed at Mainz-Finthen but the airfield was not then ready.

1 March 35	1 April 36	1 April 37	1 July 38	1 November 38
		I./JG 131[1] Jesau	I./JG 131 Jesau	I./JG 130 Jesau
I./JG 132 Döberitz	I./JG 132 Döberitz	I./JG 132 Döberitz	I./JG 132 Döberitz	I./JG 131 Döberitz
II./JG 132 Damm	II./JG 132 Damm	II./JG 132 Damm	II./JG 132 Damm	I./JG 141 Damm
			III./JG 132(2) Damm	II./JG 141 Furstenwalde
			IV./JG 132(3) Werneuchen	I./JG 331 Mähr Trubach
	I./JG 134[4] Dortmund	I./JG 134 Dortmund	I./JG 134 Dortmund	I./JG 142 Dortmund
	II./JG 134[5] Werl	II./JG 134 Werl	II./JG 134 Werl	II./JG 142 Werl
	III./JG 134 Lippstadt	II.(schwere J)/LG[6] Barth	II.(schwere J)/LG Barth	II.(schwere J)/LG Barth
			IV./JG 134[7] Dortmund	III./JG 142 Lippstadt
		I./JG 135 Bad Aibling	I./JG 135 Bad Aibling	I./JG 233 Bad Aibling
			II./JG 135[8] Bad Aibling	I./JG 333 Herzogenaurach
1 & 2./Kü.J. 136[9] Kiel-Holtenau	I./JG 136 Kiel-Holtenau	I./JG 136 Jever	I./JG 136 Jever	II./JG 333 Marienbad
		4./JG 136[10] Jever	1.(leicht J.)/LG Garz	1.(leicht J.)/LG Garz
	I./JG 232[11] Bernburg	I./JG 232 Bernburg	I./JG 137[12] Bernburg	I./JG 231 Bernburg
			II./JG 137 Zerbst	II./JG 231 Zerbst
			I./JG 138 Vienna	I./JG 134 Vienna
		I./JG 234[13] Köln	I./JG 234 Köln	I./JG 132 Köln
		II./JG 234[14] Düsseldorf	II./JG 234 Düsseldorf	II./JG 132 Düsseldorf
			III./JG 234[15] Düsseldorf	I./JG 143 Illesheim
	I./JG 334 Wiesbaden	I./JG 334 Wiesbaden	I./JG 334 Wiesbaden	I./JG 133 Wiesbaden
	II./JG 334 Mannheim	II./JG 334 Mannheim	II./JG 334 Mannheim	II./JG 133 Mannheim
			III./JG 334[16] Jesau	I./JG 144 Gablingen
				I./JG 433 Boblingen

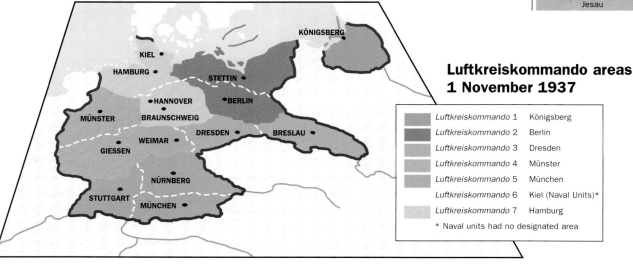

Luftkreiskommando areas 1 November 1937

	Luftkreiskommando 1	Königsberg
	Luftkreiskommando 2	Berlin
	Luftkreiskommando 3	Dresden
	Luftkreiskommando 4	Münster
	Luftkreiskommando 5	München
	Luftkreiskommando 6	Kiel (Naval Units)*
	Luftkreiskommando 7	Hamburg

* Naval units had no designated area

Unfettered Expansion

From 1937 there was no holding back, as Nazi Germany indulged itself in rapid and extensive rearmament. In February of that year, II./JG 132 received 25 examples of an ultra-modern fighter aircraft – the all-metal, low-wing Messerschmitt Bf 109 monoplane – and in doing so became the first unit in the new *Luftwaffe* to become equipped with this legendary aircraft.

Apart from receiving new equipment, three new fighter *Geschwader* were formed in March 1937, JG 135, JG 234 and JG 334. On the 15th of the month, personnel and equipment arrived at the Bavarian town of Bad Aibling to form the nucleus of I./JG 135 under *Obstlt.* Max Ibel. The unit was equipped with Ar 68s and He 51s

On the same day, elements of 8. and 9./JG 134 equipped with Ar 65s, Ar 68s and He 51s, still based at Köln-Butzweilerhof following the Rhineland operation, were used to form I./JG 234 at Köln under *Hptm.* Walter Grabmann. Just previously, on 3 March, 5./JG 134 had formed the core of II./JG 234 at Düsseldorf under *Major* Werner Rentsch. A proposal to quarter this Ar 68-equipped *Gruppe* at Bonn was abandoned due to that airfield's poor condition and state of construction. These new units were equipped with the Ar 68 and later, in mid-1938, were scheduled to receive the new Bf 109 C. The remaining elements of III./JG 134 then moved back to their original base at Lippstadt for a short period before moving again to Barth on the Baltic coast to become the II.(*schwere Jagd*)/LG – *Lehrgeschwader.*

Following a decree issued by Göring in March 1936, the *Geschwaderstab* and I./JG 334 was established from elements of I./JG 134 at the former racetrack of Wiesbaden-Erbenheim and II./JG 334 from elements of I./JG 132 at Mannheim-Sandhofen. The *Kommodore* was *Oberst* Bruno Loerzer (who had moved from I./JG 232) and amongst the pilots of the First *Gruppe* in March 1937 were young officers who would later rise to stardom as aces of the war-time *Jagdwaffe: Oblt.* Werner Mölders *(Staffelkapitän* of 2./JG 334), *Oblt.* Wolfgang Lippert, *Lt.* Rolf Pingel and *Lt.* Josef Priller. The *Geschwader* was equipped with the Ar 68. During the first months of its existence, the component units of JG 334, like many of the other newly-formed German fighter units, practised formation flying, navigation and air-firing. Exercises took place in the Friesland and Hamburg areas and in early 1938, the unit took delivery of the new Bf 109 B and D variants. For the pilots, conversion over to this new type of fighter involved a major adjustment in control techniques.

A little later, on 1 April 1937, another *Gruppe*, I./JG 131 was formed at Jüterbog-Damm from a nucleus provided by II./JG 132. Shortly afterwards the unit moved to Jesau in East Prussia being equipped with the Ar 68 F. The unit's *Kommandeur* was *Hptm.* Bernhard Woldenga. A second *Gruppe* of JG 131 – to be based at Prowehren – remained at the planning stage only.

All this rapid expansion led to a re-organisation of the six Regional Air Commands on 12 October 1937. The boundaries of *Luftkreiskommando* 2, 4 and 5 (now being identified by Arabic numbers) were changed and a seventh Command created with its headquarters in Hamburg. The term Air Office or *Luftamt* had already been abandoned (on 1 April 1936) and replaced by Area Air Commands or *Luftgaukommando* identified by Roman numerals.

In November 1937 the Second Gruppe of JG 234, now under the command of *Obstlt.* Eduard von Schleich, received its first Bf 109 Bs, the second *Geschwader* to equip with the new fighter. On 1 November 1938, Schleich, now an *Oberst,* became the first *Kommodore* of the *Geschwader* which was simultaneously renamed JG 132. On 11 December 1938, the unit received the honorary title "*Jagdgeschwader Schlageter*" after Albert Leo Schlageter, a nationalist hero.

The re-arrangement of the *Luftkreiskommando* resulted in the redesignation of I./JG 232 as I./JG 137, the *Gruppe* now under the leadership of *Hptm.* Hannes Gentzen. On 1 February 1938, the He 51B-equipped components of I./JG 137 were integrated into I.(*leicht Jagd*)/LG – *Lehrgeschwader* and transferred to Garz, leaving on 1./JG 137 at Bernburg. By 1 October 1938, the unit had been expanded back to full *Gruppe* strength.

On 13 March 1938, Austria was incorporated into Germany, an eighth *Luftkreiskommando* being established with its headquarters in Vienna. The new command emcompassed the whole of Austria except for the Tyrol which was placed within the boundaries of *Luftkreiskommando* 5. Shortly afterwards some of the the six Austrian fighter squadrons, equipped in the main with Italian Fiat C.R.32 biplanes, formed the basis of a new *Luftwaffe Gruppe* known as I./JG 138, with others being incorporated into JG 135. Based at Vienna-Aspern I./JG 138 was placed under the command of *Hptm.* Wilfried Müller-Rienzburg and re-equipped with Ar 68s. In the former Austrian Air Force's commander, *General* Alexander Löhr, the *Luftwaffe* was also to gain one of its most able leaders, and two of Germany's most famous fighter pilots, *Oberst* Gordon Gollob and *Major* Walter Nowotny also came from the country.

ABOVE: A line-up of factory fresh Bf 109 Bs after delivery to II./JG 132. The superb Messerschmitt fighter began to replace the He 51 and Ar 68 in Luftwaffe service from the spring of 1937. Its introduction brought a change to Jagdwaffe camouflage, all Bf 109s of the period having black-green (RLM colour 70) and dark green (71) uppersurfaces with pale blue (65) undersurfaces.

RIGHT: The introduction of the new all-metal Bf 109 B-1 fighter into Luftwaffe service during the summer of 1937 brought with it a new upper surface camouflage pattern in two shades of green, 70 and 71. At first, the black Hakenkreuz on a white circle superimposed on a red band nationality marking was retained painted across the fin and rudder. The positioning of the white number 8 aft of the fuselage Balkenkreuz on this aircraft was unusual.

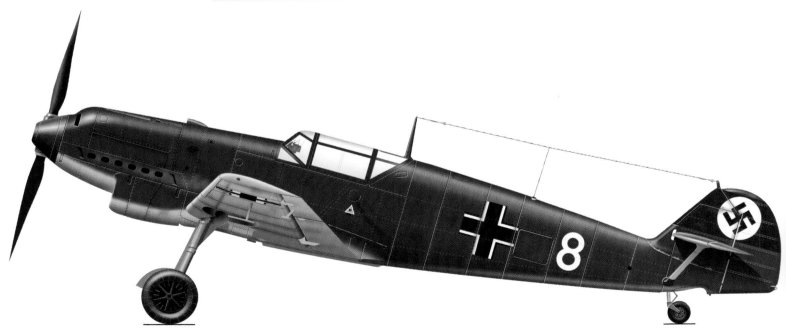

Messerschmitt Bf 109 B-2 of 1./JG 133
Based at Wiesbaden-Erbenheim, winter 1938-39. Although the aircraft of the First Gruppe of JG 133 employed similar camouflage to the Bf 109s of the 6. Staffel illustrated elsewhere, they were unusual in that the individual number was painted aft of the fuselage Balkenkreuz.

On 1 July 1938, no fewer than seven new *Jagdgruppen* were formed; III. and IV./JG 132, IV./JG 134, II./JG 135, II./JG 137, III./JG 234 and III./JG 334. III./JG 132 was formed at Damm under *Maj.Dr.-Ing.* Ernst Bormann, but moved to *Fürstenwalde* shortly afterwards. IV./JG 132 was established from elements of the recently-formed *Jagdfliegerschule Werneuchen* which was moved to Oschatz under the command of *Obstlt.* Theo Osterkamp. It was the only front line *Luftwaffe* unit to be equipped with the He 112. Osterkamp was a former First World War *Pour le Mérite* holder and *Oblt.* Hannes Trautloft, who would go on to win the *Ritterkreuz* and become one of the *Jagdwaffe's* most respected tactical commanders, led 12. Staffel.

IV./JG 134 was formed at Dortmund under *Hptm.* Schalk, comprising three *Staffeln* and equipped with the Ar 68. II./JG 135 was formed at Bad Aibling under *Major* Stoltenhoff, but this unit was composed initially of just one *Staffel* of Ar 68s. II./JG 137 was formed at Zerbst under *Major* von Houwald and III./JG 234 was created at Düsseldorf under Hptm. Lessmann, but transferred to Schweidnitz in November. III./JG 334 was formed at Mannheim-Sandhofen under *Hptm.* Schmidt-Coste and was equipped, unlike the rest of the *Geschwader,* with the Ar 68.

Previously, on 4 February 1938 another reshuffle had taken place among the *Luftwaffe* areas of command. The seven *Luftkreiskommando* had been abandoned and replaced by three *Luftwaffengruppenkommando* plus three *Luftwaffenkommando* to co-ordinate operations in East Prussia, Austria and at sea. These units and their headquarters were:

Luftwaffenkommando Ost Preussen	Königsberg
Luftgau I	Königsberg
Luftwaffengruppenkommando 1	Berlin
Luftgau III	Berlin
Luftgau IV	Dresden
Luftgau VIII	Breslau
Luftwaffengruppenkommando 2	Braunschweig
Luftgau VI	Münster
Luftgau XI	Hannover
Luftwaffengruppenkommando 3	München
Luftgau VII	Berlin
Luftgau XII	Stuttgart
Luftgau XIII	Wiesbaden
Luftwaffenkommando Österreich	Vienna
Luftgau XVII	Vienna
Luftwaffenkommando See	Kiel

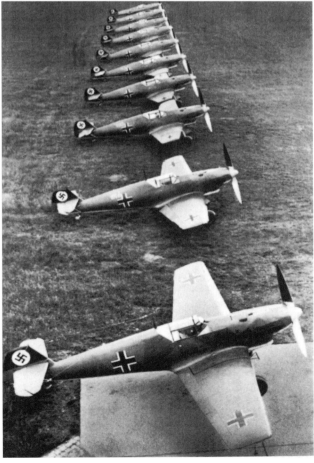

BELOW: When the first 25 Bf 109 B-1s were delivered to II./JG 132 "Richthofen" in February 1937, they were fitted with the large wooden fixed two-bladed propeller and were camouflaged in black-green and dark green. They were however to retain the early style Balkenkreuz national insignia with thin white outlines and black edging. They also carried the original black Hakenkreuz on a white circle painted over a red tail band.

By November 1938, the potential of the Bf 110 twin-engined fighter had prompted the *Luftwaffe* to create a number of heavy fighter units which, it was hoped, would be the first to be re-equipped with the new aircraft. The middle figure in the unit designation was changed from a "3" to a "4", and the units later received the prefix "ZG" for *Zerstörergeschwader* (destroyer wings). This event, and the reorganisation of the areas of command which had taken place earlier in the year, led to a wholesale redesignation of the *Jagdwaffe*. The last figure of the unit designation for Gruppen operating under the *Kommando* in East Prussia was changed to "0", those under *Gruppenkommando* 1 to 3 to "1" to "3" respectively and those under the *Kommando* in Vienna to "4". These redesignations are detailed in Appendix 1. The only new *Jagdgruppe* to be formed at this time was I./JG 433 at Böblingen.

On 1 February 1939 the beginnings of the *Luftwaffe's* night fighter force was established when 10.(NJ)/JG 131 was formed at Döberitz. Equipped with the Ar 68 this unit was the first of several to initiate experimental night-fighter operations.

LEFT AND OPPOSITE: During the spring of 1937, the first Bf 109 B-1s were delivered to JG 132 "Richthofen" under Oberst Gerd von Massow. This was the first production model of a fighter with which, more than any other aircraft, the name of Messerschmitt, is associated. These photographs show "Red 3" of 5./JG 132 with the famous "script R" badge of the Geschwader beneath the cockpit.

LEFT: Pilots of JG 132 receive their first batch of Messerschmitt Bf 109 Bs and are congratulated by senior officers. The tall individual, shaking hands second from left, wearing pilots' overalls, is Hannes Trautloft. Note that the Bf 109 in the picture does not yet carry any unit markings.

BELOW: On 20 June 1937 the Luftwaffe was invited to participate in a "Flying Day" to be held at Budapest-Budaörs Airport to celebrate its official opening. One of the main attractions was the attendance of German, Italian and Austrian warplanes. The Luftwaffe sent a Staffel of Bf 109 Bs from JG 132 "Richthofen", the Austrians and Italians with FIAT CR-32s, the latter also bringing along a few Savoia-Marchetti S.M.-79 bombers. The Hungarians participated with a civilian aerobatic team (officially there was no Hungarian airforce at that time), and a few Ju 52 paratroop carriers. The Luftwaffe sent some its most experienced fighter pilots: Oblt. von Müller Reim, Hptm. Lothar von Janson, Lt. Klein, Fw. Göecke (?), Lt. Thier, Oblt. Paul Panske, Oblt. Hannes Trautloft, Oblt. Herwig Knüppel, Lt. Dietrich von Bothmer, Oblt. Günther Radusch and Oblt. Hennig Strümpell. They presented their brand new Bf 109 Bs which sported the red horizontal tail band with the black Hakenkreuz on a white circle, as well as older He 51s and Ju 52s. Wearing their white summer uniform jackets, from the right: Lt. von Bothmer, Oblt. Strümpell, unknown, Oblt. Trautloft, Oblt. Radusch (with back to camera) and in standard uniform, wearing the "Richthofen" arm-band, Hptm. von Janson. In the background are the first of the unit's Bf 109 Bs together with their previous He 51s and two Ju 52/3m transports. The nearest Bf 109 B carries the individual number "5" (probably in red) behind the Balkenkreuz. As the first unit to be re-equipped with the Bf 109, II./JG 132 sometimes had the aircraft identification number painted between the fuselage Balkenkreuz and the tail. This practice was to change with the issuing by the Luftwaffe Generalstab of directive Fl.In.3 Nr.730/37 II on 14 December 1937. This called for the numbers to be applied to both fuselage sides forward of the fuselage Balkenkreuz.

ABOVE: This black-green (70) and dark green (71) camouflaged Bf 109 provides a comfortable bed for a pilot of II./JG 132. The bulge directly above his head is the supercharger air intake.

Geschwader "Richthofen" badge

Messerschmitt Bf 109 B-2 of 5./JG 132 "Richthofen"
Depicted at Jüterbog-Damm, summer 1937. II./JG 132 was the first unit to
receive the Bf 109, the aircraft being delivered in black-green (70) and dark
green (71) camouflage with pale blue (65) beneath. The red outlined in white
individual number and horizontal bar of the second Gruppe appear exactly as
laid down in the directive of 14 December 1937.

1937-1938

RIGHT: This He 51 has been jacked up to allow armourers to re-synchronise the two fixed forward-firing 7.9 mm MG 17 machines guns. Each weapon carried 500 rounds.

BELOW: This Ar 68 E-1 was flown by Lt. Böhmel and carried the markings of 7./JG 132 but probably belonged to 4./JG 141 from which it was formed on 1 November 1938. At this time, some Ar 68s began to receive the black-green (70) and dark green (71) camouflage with pale blue (65) beneath. The aircraft carried the white number "6" and a white wavy line, which indicated that the aircraft belonged to the third Gruppe.

BELOW: By 1 April 1937 six new Jagdgruppen were formed within the Luftwaffe, I./JG 131, I./JG 135, I. and II./JG 234 and I. and II./JG 334. One of these groups, I./JG 135, was established at Bad Aibling south-east of München. To commemorate the event the city held a ceremony with slogans such as: "Bad Aibling grüßt Seine Flieger" ("Bad Aibling salutes its flyers"). I./JG 135 was eventually to become I./JG 51 in May 1939.

LEFT: Major Max Ibel, the first Gruppenkommandeur of I./JG 135 at the ceremony establishing his unit at Bad Aibling. Ibel was one of the German pilots trained at Lipezk in Russia and was appointed commander of I./JG 135 after having served as a Staffelkapitän in I./JG 232. He later became Kommodore of JG 27, being awarded the Ritterkreuz on 22 August 1940. In June 1941 he was appointed to lead various Jagdfliegerführer and from September 1943 to February 1945 was commander of the 2.Jagddivision.

LEFT AND ABOVE: Mechanics posing in front of of a line-up of He 51 B-1s belonging to 3./JG 135 at Bad Aibling. Note the Gruppe emblem, just visible, on the aircraft in the foreground and the pale blue engine cowling and upper fuselage decking.

"He called us "Grey Wolves"…"

GÜNTHER SCHOLZ

"During 1931/32, I flew as a *Sportflieger,* a sports flier with the DLV 11 whose president was Bruno Loerzer, but the employment situation was so bad during 1932-33 that I decided to join the armed forces. At that time it was easier to join the *Kriegsmarine* (German Navy) because the *Luftwaffe* was still only in its infancy. I signed up on 8 April 1934 at Stralsund and was inducted into the *Marineschule*. Whilst there, I met the future fighter ace and later NATO General, Johannes Steinhoff who was, at that time, a warrant officer. Always hoping to fly again, it was not long before I asked for a transfer to the new *Luftwaffe*. Wearing my blue navy uniform, and with the rank of *Fähnrich,* I went to Salzwedel to commence my flying training. As I already had my civilian A-2 licence to fly light aircraft and could perform basic aerobatics, I expected my training to be shorter than that the rest of my comrades.

"It was therefore not long before I was sent to *Jagdgruppe Bernburg* commanded by Bruno Loerzer, with Adolf Galland as Technical Officer. My *Staffelkapitän, Oblt.* Wolfgang Schellmann, would also become famous in the years that followed. In March 1937 our unit formed the basis of a new fighter *Gruppe* known as I./JG 135. I belonged to the *"Vorkommando"*, which commisioned the *Gruppe's* new airfield at Bad Aibling. At this time our officers and men were billeted in hotels in the village, but we were not popular as no-one wanted a military presence in the area. In fact, as soon as we appeared, the population would disappear into their houses because the local Catholic priest had warned them about the "grey wolves" as he called us. The young ladies were not so reticent, however, and this helped to end the distrust. Our *Kommandeur* at this time was *Major* Ibel and our *Staffelkapitäne* were *Oberleutnante* Andres, Brustellin and Schellmann with Hannes Trautloft and Dietrich Hrabak arriving later.

"Then, in early 1937, fighter pilots were asked to go to Spain. Nearly all unmarried pilots were ready and eager to go. In my case, I wanted to see some action and experience lots of exciting adventures, but perhaps the most important thing was that we would have the opportunity to fly some of the most powerful aircraft of the time. Last but not least, the pay was high, around 1,200 *Reichsmarks* a month for a *Leutnant*! When I returned to Germany, I was able to do what most of my comrades did and buy a fantastic car."

RIGHT: Belonging to I./JG 135, this in-flight photo of an He 51 B-1 is most unusual in that it carries the code 51+D14. This would indicate an aircraft of the fourth Staffel of the first Gruppe, but these were not added to Luftwaffe fighter units until the middle of 1944.

ABOVE: The first fighter delivered to 2./JG 135 at Bad Aibling was the He 51 B, this variant differing from the A-series in having increased undercarriage bracing and provision for a 170 litre (37.5 Imp gal) drop tank. JG 135 had the cowlings and upper fuselage decking of their aircraft painted pale blue, with white bands around the engine and rear fuselage in white indicating the second Staffel.

RIGHT: As far as is known, only three Luftwaffe fighter units used the five character code system before this was replaced by numbers and symbols during the autumn of 1936. These were JG 132 which used "21" as the first numbers in their code, JG 135 which used "51" and JG 136 which used "60". This aircraft from 3./JG 135 was badly damaged in a landing accident. The wing of the aircraft can be seen in the background.

LEFT: This He 51 of 1./JG 135 probably carries the code 51+B11 before the unit adopted the more familiar sequence of "Traditional Colours", numbers and symbols. The aircraft also carries the Gruppe emblem below the cockpit and has a white stripe painted on one propeller blade.

Heinkel He 51 B-1 of 1./JG 135

Depicted at Bad Aibling, autumn 1937. Rather out of step with other Luftwaffe fighter units of the period, the aircraft carries the five character code 51+K11 but with the pale blue "Traditional Colour" engine cowling and upper fuselage decking.

Badge of 1./JG 135 and later 1./JG 233 "Kitzbüheler Gams".

ABOVE AND RIGHT: After the Anschluss many pilots from the old Austrian Air Force were incorporated into I./JG 135, the painting of the "Kitzbüheler Gams" (Kitzbühel Goat) badge on the fuselage sides commemorating this fact. The Kitzbühel Alps are a mountain range in the Austrian Tyrol.

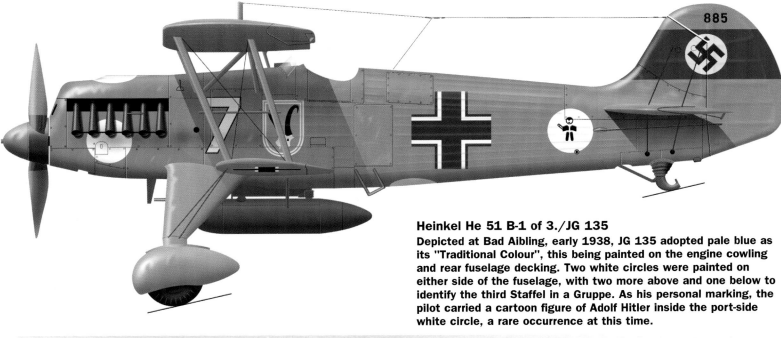

Heinkel He 51 B-1 of 3./JG 135

Depicted at Bad Aibling, early 1938, JG 135 adopted pale blue as its "Traditional Colour", this being painted on the engine cowling and rear fuselage decking. Two white circles were painted on either side of the fuselage, with two more above and one below to identify the third Staffel in a Gruppe. As his personal marking, the pilot carried a cartoon figure of Adolf Hitler inside the port-side white circle, a rare occurrence at this time.

ABOVE: A neat line-up of He 51s of 3./JG 135 photographed at Bad Aibling near München. These aircraft all have white circles painted on the pale blue fuselage decking and on a similarly coloured band around the rear fuselage. This marking identified the third Staffel within a Gruppe, the Gruppen themselves being recognised by no additional marking (I. Gruppe), a horizontal bar painted below the cockpit (II. Gruppe) or a wavy line in the same position (III. Gruppe). Variations of these symbols were used throughout the Second World War.

RIGHT: The third Staffel of each fighter Gruppe was identified by a large white circle painted on both sides of the engine cowling as well as on both sides of the rear fuselage. The same marking also appeared above the rear fuselage decking and beneath the lower wing centre section. These two aircraft, "White 1" and "White 6" photographed in spring 1937 probably belonged to JG 134.

RIGHT: Photographed in 1937, this Kette of Ar 68 Fs of 6./JG 135 are shown in flight over Bavaria. The angle of the camera shows to advantage the position of the aircraft's individual number painted underneath, as well as on both sides of the fuselage. It was also repeated on the top of the wing centre section. Shortly after its formation, II./JG 135 moved from Bad Aibling to Straubing and then Herzogenaurach.

Arado Ar 68 E-1 of 3./JG 135
Depicted at Bad Aibling, late 1938. The white "7" thinly outlined in black with white circles painted on both sides of the fuselage identified an aircraft of the third Staffel. It was not unusual for the wheel spats to be removed to ease maintenance.

LEFT: Parked beneath the trees, this Ar 68 E was operated by 3./JG 135 at Bad Aibling. I./JG 135 was redesignated I./JG 233 in November 1938 and I./JG 51 in May 1939 at which point it operated Bf 109s.

RIGHT: During the mid 1930s the fighters of the fledgling Luftwaffe were still flying in groups of three known as the Kette. Following operational experience in Spain, this was to change to elements of two (the Rotte) which was doubled up to four (the Schwarm) of four aircraft.

LEFT: Two brand new He 51 A-1s still carrying their white factory code numbers. The fuselage crosses are lacking the black edging to the white surround.

LEFT: Most He 51s were transferred to training units when the fighter units were re-equipped with the Bf 109. Here a He 51 B coded BX+NI, with a Fw 56 *Stösser* (Hawk) behind, are shown in typical training unit markings. This variant of He 51 had a strengthened fuselage and undercarriage. Note also the absence of wheel spats which made it easier to take-off and land on muddy airfields.

LEFT: This Kette of He 51s carry the white stripe marking around the engine cowling and rear fuselage indicating they belonged to the 2./Staffel of a fighter unit.

RIGHT: Three Ketten of He 51s of I./JG 135 practice formation flying over the Bavarian countryside during 1937.

BELOW: Bad Aibling, late 1937. Three Leutnante from 3./JG 135 pose in front of their He 51s. All three were to achieve fame with the wartime Luftwaffe. They are, from left to right: Günther Scholz, Wolfgang Schellmann and Herbert Kijewski. Kijewski, who rose to become a Major, and Kommandeur of II./JG 1 was killed on 16 April 1943 when his Fw 190 A-5 was shot down near Vlissingen. Schellmann was promoted to Major but was killed on 22 June 1941 as Kommodore of JG 27. Scholz commanded JG 5 from June 1943 to the end of the war, reaching the rank of Oberstleutnant.

RIGHT: With its engine running Uffz. Hugo Dahmer's He 51 B, "White 4" of I./JG 234, prepares for take-off from Düsseldorf in 1938. The absence of any additional markings around the orange fuselage decking indicates that the aircraft was operated by the first Staffel.

ABOVE AND RIGHT: As can be seen in these photos, often the aircraft individual numbers were repeated above the centre section of the top wing in addition to being painted just forward of the cockpit and beneath the fuselage centre section. These He 51s were used by I./JG 135 at Bad Aibling. An unusual feature is that many of them carry a dark coloured second Gruppe symbol, probably in black.

ABOVE: This excellent photo shows off the lines of He 51 B-1 "White 8" of 3./JG 135 coming in to land at Bad Aibling

LEFT: Mechanics watch as the BMW VI engine of this He 51 of 3./JG 135 is run up during a routine maintenance session. This photo gives an excellent view of the various engine access covers.

RIGHT: This group of seven He 51 B-1s of 3./JG 135 at Bad Aibling had pale blue engine cowlings and upper fuselage top decking, but unlike the photograph on page 64 opposite, they do not have their individual numbers repeated above the top wing centre section.

ABOVE: Two He 51s of I./JG 135 photographed at Bad Aibling during the spring of 1937. The white chevron and vertical bar on the He 51 to the right signifies that it was the third aircraft in the Stabskette, flown in this case by the Gruppenadjutant, Oblt. Hans Schmoller-Haldy. The aircraft "White 7" carries a white band around the nose and rear fuselage indicating that it belonged to 3. Staffel.

BELOW: This He 51 B-1 of 3./JG 135 has its engine cowling finished in pale blue, a similar colour being used to paint the forward half of the spinner. The centre of the propeller was finished in varnished polished wood, but the blades were painted pale grey (63) with the Schwarz company's logo on the front of each blade.

ABOVE: The Ar 68 F could easily be distinguished from its Jumo powered counterpart by its much more bulky engine installation. The variant was delivered to the Luftwaffe from the summer of 1936, first to I./JG 134 at Dortmund and later to I./JG 131 at Jesau. It had been hoped that the Ar 68 would supersede the He 51 but trials conducted between the two aircraft by Ernst Udet proved that the former did not have much of an improved performance, but was easier to maintain.

LEFT: At the "Justierstand" (stabilising platform). To calibrate the twin 7.9 mm MG 17 machine guns, a disc was temporarily fitted in place of the propeller and the aircraft jacked up for firing trials. Armament had changed little since the end of the First World War when virtually all fighter aircraft carried two machine-guns synchronised to fire through the propeller. When the first Bf 109 Bs were delivered they had a third gun mounted between the cylinder rows of the engine firing through the spinner, and later variants introduced first wing mounted machine-guns and later 20 mm cannon

LEFT: Contact! Two mechanics swing the propeller of this Ar 68 F in order to start its BMW VI engine. It would appear that the cowling for the cooling system is open in this photo.

RIGHT: As part of their training, fighter pilots flew regular attacks on specially rigged ground targets. Here a He 51 dives at a target in a simulated ground attack.

BELOW: A hive of activity as a Staffel of Ar 68 Es is readied for take-off. Only two production versions of the Arado fighter saw service with the Luftwaffe; the Ar 68 E with a Jumo 210 engine and the Ar 68 F with a BMW VI. Two later variants were however proposed, the Ar 68 G with a supercharged BMW in-line engine and the Ar 68 H with a 850 hp BMW 132 radial engine and an enclosed cockpit.

RIGHT: The white circles painted on the engine cowling and rear tail band of this Ar 68 F identify the aircraft as belonging to the 3. Staffel of one of the early Jagdgeschwadern. The colour of the cowling and upper fuselage decking would identify the unit - either black for JG 131, red for JG 132, brown for JG 134, pale blue for JG 135, green for JG 232 (later JG 137) or orange for JG 234.

This series of photos show Jumo 210 powered Ar 68 Es of a Luftwaffe fighter unit which has yet to be identified but may have been I./JG 334 which later became I./JG 133. Like all contemporary He 51s and Ar 68s the aircraft were given a primer coat of oil based light grey, an undercoat of silver and a final coat of grey which had a green cast to it. Service areas for foot traffic were finished in gloss black. The finish produced a definite glossy sheen to the surfaces which emphasises that the scheme was not intended for camouflage purposes. While this colouring was not initially intended for camouflage purposes it, it did become incorporated into the first fully developed camouflage scheme as RLM colour 63. It is interesting to note that the white individual numbers painted on the aircraft in these photos have no black outline.

ABOVE AND RIGHT: This Ar 68 E-1 had a white circle painted on both sides of the engine cowling and repeated on the rear fuselage which indicated that they belonged to the third Staffel. Possibly operated by 3./JG 334 or 3./JG 133 which does not appear to have carried the coloured engine cowlings adopted by other contemporary German fighter units.

LEFT: These Ar 68 E-1s were probably operated by 3./JG 334 some of whose aircraft are thought to have had coloured upper fuselage decking.

"The thing that mattered above all else was that I could fly…"

WINFRIED SCHMIDT

Winfried Schmidt was accredited with claiming one of the *Jagdwaffe's* earliest victories against the RAF when he shot down a Wellington bomber over the North Sea on 18 December 1939. He then went on to score a further 18 victories in some 150 missions whilst with II./JG 77 and III./JG 3. He was wounded three times during operations over the Western Front and on a further occasion over Russia whilst *Staffelkapitän* with 8./JG 3 after which he was assigned to Staff duties.

"I was born in Köln on 18 February 1915. During the 1920s, we experienced very difficult times in Germany, with famine and poverty. As with many of the young, I tried to forget these depressing times by playing games and sport. We refought the First World War and relived the exploits of our aces - men such as von Richthofen, Boelcke and Immelmann. The intense adulation of these men did not diminish during the post-war years and in fact was kept alive by the progressive ascent into power by men such as Hermann Göring. But I also had a hobby which linked me very closely to the world of aviation; I built scale models of aircraft which I was gradually able to motorise.

"By 1933, I had the opportunity to fly in gliders which I really enjoyed. The following year, I joined a private aviation club which soon became incorporated into the *Deutscher Luftsport Verband* (DLV) - the German Air Sport association - formed at that time to promote public interest in aeromodelling, gliding, balloons and powered aircraft as well as to form the basis of a new *Luftwaffe*. As a member of this club and with financial assistance from my father, I had the opportunity to win my A1 and A2 certificates, the latter allowing me to pilot single-engined aircraft to carry a passenger.

"As we were still civilians, we normally flew the Klemm 25. This aircraft was so light and slow that we were not authorised to take off if the weather was too windy!

"In the autumn of 1935, I had to do my *Reichs Arbeitsdienst* - Reich Labour Service - and so I had to spend a year working unpaid for the State, which would be followed by one year of military service. However, in order to avoid spending too many months "penniless", I decided to volunteer for the Army for that was the best way to avoid *Reichs Arbeitsdienst*. I was fortunate because at that very moment the *Luftwaffe* was being rebuilt - despite the terms of the Treaty of Versailles. Naturally, I chose the *Luftwaffe*.

"I attended different training schools such as the general training school at Schleißheim where I was able to fly the Arado Ar 66. However, since it was my intention to become a fighter pilot, I began to fly aircraft which lent themselves to that type of deployment such as the Arado Ar 65 biplane.

"I was finally designated a "fighter pilot" in 1937. At the beginning of 1938 with the rank of *Gefreiter*, I was posted to a newly formed *Geschwader*, JG 334 based at Frankfurt-Rebstock. I was assigned to 2./JG 334 whose *Staffelkapitän* was Werner Mölders, later to become one of the most outstanding personalities of the German fighter arm. But if my *Staffelkapitän* had yet to win fame, this was not the case for our *Kommodore* who was one of the First World War aces who had often figured in my childhood games; *Oberst* Bruno Loerzer had been awarded *Pour le Mérite* for his 44 victories during the First World War. My *Gruppenkommandeur, Major* Hans-Hugo Witt, was also well known but for tragic reasons, since he was one of the few survivors from the *Graf Zeppelin* balloon catastrophe.

"Among the young pilots whom I met in that *Gruppe* were - apart from Mölders - many others who would later enjoy successful service careers in the *Jagdwaffe*; Josef Priller, Rolf Pingel, Hubertus von Bonin, Wolfgang Lippert and Franz Götz.

"My relations with Mölders were excellent and from the beginning he had always said to me that I would not stay a *Gefreiter* for long; "I had to become an officer"!

"Mölders trained our *Staffel* - which was later based at Wiesbaden-Erbenheim airfield - very well, teaching us different types of flight formation. With our Arado Ar 68s, we simulated combat and fired against ground targets as well as sandbags trailed through the sky.

"We received some Bf 108s and soon after that, the Bf 109. It was a revelation to us. A fantastic aircraft!

"At around that time, our *Staffel* was regularly depleted of pilots who had been ordered to Spain. It happened to Mölders in April 1938; he handed the unit over to *Hptm*. Rolf Pingel (who had just got back from Spain). Pingel also insisted that I should seriously consider becoming an officer, but the prospect didn't appeal to me very much. As far as being in the *Luftwaffe* was concerned, the thing that mattered above all else was that I could fly as readily and as cheaply as I could. I eventually elected to become a reserve officer and thus had to remain in the *Luftwaffe* for several more months. In October 1938, as a *Leutnant der Reserve*, I left the service in order commence study as a technical engineer at Aachen. I did not know that peace would be so abruptly ended so that I would only spend one year at university. Indeed, in the summer of 1939, I was recalled to the *Luftwaffe* and posted to the German Bight area, attached to *Oblt*. von Lojewski's 5./JG 77."

RIGHT: Rolf Pingel photographed just after his return from Spain and shortly after taking command of 2./JG 334.

BELOW IN BOX: A group of pilots from II./JG 334 with a three-seat Heinkel He 70 F-2 reconnaissance aircraft of 1.(F)/124 - the 1st (long-range) Staffel of Reconnaissance Gruppe 124 in the background. The pilots are, from left to right: (unknown), Lt. Böhner (later with 6./JG 53), Fw. Eichel, Lt. Finsterbusch (later with 5./JG 53) and Fw. Hellge (later with 6./JG 53 - killed on 22 September 1939).

"Our duty was to watch the border with France..."

OTTO BÖHNER

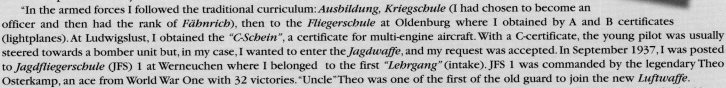

Otto Böhner was to have an exemplary career in the *Luftwaffe*, being appointed *Staffelkapitän* of 6./JG 53. He spent the last two years of the war as a *Staffelkapitän* in JG 400, the only *Geschwader* to be equipped with the Me 163 rocket fighter.

"I was born in Hamburg on 14 December 1913. After the First World War, I began technical studies at the High Schools at Berlin and Rostock. In the early 1930s I had the opportunity to learn flying during my studies and, in 1934, I obtained my first flight certificate. Shortly after this the new *Luftwaffe* was officially revealed and the armed forces displayed a great interest in all young men who had a flight certificate. I was therefore contacted and decided to accept the offer and enter the armed forces. This was in April 1935. This option permitted me to avoid the many weapons exercises and drill and thus I could start my main ambition as soon as possible - to fly.

"In the armed forces I followed the traditional curriculum: *Ausbildung, Kriegschule* (I had chosen to become an officer and then had the rank of *Fähnrich*), then to the *Fliegerschule* at Oldenburg where I obtained by A and B certificates (lightplanes). At Ludwigslust, I obtained the *"C-Schein"*, a certificate for multi-engine aircraft. With a C-certificate, the young pilot was usually steered towards a bomber unit but, in my case, I wanted to enter the *Jagdwaffe*, and my request was accepted. In September 1937, I was posted to *Jagdfliegerschule* (JFS) 1 at Werneuchen where I belonged to the first *"Lehrgang"* (intake). JFS 1 was commanded by the legendary Theo Osterkamp, an ace from World War One with 32 victories. "Uncle" Theo was one of the first of the old guard to join the new *Luftwaffe*.

"It was at this school that I performed my first fighter pilot flight with my teacher, another legendary figure, Hannes Trautloft, who had been trained at Lipezk in Russia. In April 1938, having completed my training, I was posted with the rank of *Leutnant* to the newly created II./JG 334 at Mannheim-Sandhofen.

"Our first *Gruppe* was at Wiesbaden-Erbenheim while a third *Gruppe* was created later (on 1 July 1938 at Mannheim-Sandhofen). In our second *Gruppe*, 4./JG 334 was commanded by *Hptm.* Walter Schmidt-Coste, 5./JG 334 by *Oblt.* Kurt Fischer and 6./JG 334 by a certain *Oblt.* Günther *Freiherr* von Maltzahn ... who would have an exemplary career in the *Luftwaffe*. When I joined the unit, it was still equipped in the main with the Ar 68 - a beautiful aircraft, easy to handle and very sensitive. This followed the He 51, a very similar aeroplane. It is difficult to say which was the best, they were very similar. It mainly depended on the engine. The Ar 68 was powered by a Jumo, the He 51 by a BMW. The Messerschmitt 109 began to be delivered shortly after my arrival at JG 334. This aircraft was quite different: less to handle in the turn, but much more powerful. Its arrival made us change our tactics. Earlier we were taught to *"Einkurven"* in air combat, but with the Bf 109, the tactic used was based more upon the engine-power and speed.

"During 1938 we lived through many changes in our pilot structure. Many were sent to Spain or were posted back to our *Gruppe* after their "Spanish tour". This was the case for *Oblt.* Alfred von Lojewski (*Staffelkapitän* of 4./JG 334), *Lt.* Heinz Bretnütz (later to be appointed *Kapitän* of 6./JG 334) or *Lt.* Hubert Kroeck.

"Our *Gruppe* remained based in the west so we were not involved in events like the Austrian *Anschlu*ss the operation in *Tschekei* (Czechoslovakia). Our duty was watch the border with France and we launched all out patrols in a westerly direction."

ABOVE AND ABOVE RIGHT: This formation of Ar 68 Es is unusual in that its aircraft have coloured upper fuselage decking but this colour is not extended to the engine cowling. It is possible that the aircraft were flown by JG 334 which, unlike other contemporary Luftwaffe fighter units apparently had no official "Traditional Colour" allocated to it. One can only speculate on the shade used on the fuselage decking.

ABOVE: A group of mechanics carry out a routine service on an Ar 68 E of 1./JG 334 at Wiesbaden-Erbenheim during March 1938. Although JG 334, which later became JG 133, was equipped with Arados at this time, the unit appears not to have had coloured cowlings and upper fuselage decking as did most of the older fighter units.

LEFT AND INSET: Following a decree issued by Göring in March 1937, I./JG 334 was established from elements of I./JG 134 at the former racetrack of Wiesbaden-Erbenheim and equipped with the Ar 68 E. Unlike the other main fighter units operational at this time, (JG 131, JG 132, JG 134, JG 135, JG 232 and JG 234), JG 334 did not have coloured engine cowlings but it is possible that the upper fuselage decking was painted another colour. JG 334 was successively redesignated JG 133 and JG 53.

LEFT: The first intake or "Lehrgang", of Jagdfliegerschule 1 at Werneuchen pose in front of one of their Ar 68 E-1s at Werneuchen during the autumn of 1937. Sitting, second from the left, is Leutnant Otto Böhner with the Jagdlehrer, Oblt. Hannes Trautloft sixth from left with Walter Jänisch next left again.

BELOW: Apparently carrying no individual markings at all, this Ar 68 E-1 had probably just been delivered to JG 334. This unit was unusual in that only the fuselage top decking but not the engine cowlings of its aircraft were painted in a "Traditional Colour", the shade of which is unknown.

BELOW AND BELOW RIGHT: During 1937 a series of war games was held in Germany. For these, the wing and fuselage Balkenkreuz of certain aircraft were temporarily overpainted with red circles in order to represent the "Red Force." These two Ar 68 E-1s, which were operated by I./JG 334, were damaged while attempting a landing in soft ground. The opposing formation was known as the "Blue Force."

Arado Ar 68 E-1 of 1./JG 334
Based at Frankfurt-Rebstock, summer 1937, this aircraft has temporary red circles painted over its fuselage and wing Balkenkreuz in connection with manoeuvres held during the summer of 1937. This aircraft belonged to the "Red Force".

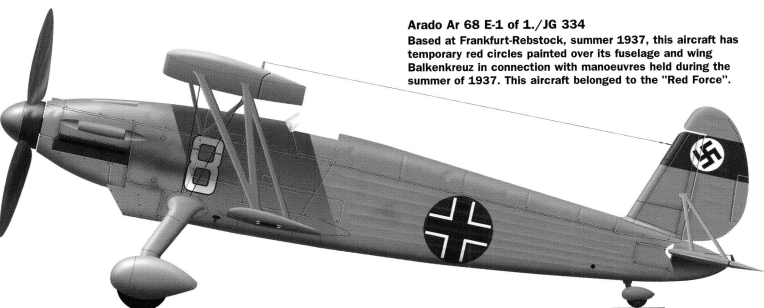

Arado Ar 68 F-1 of 3./JG 131
At Jesau in East Prussia, 1937, JG 131 used the "Traditional Colour" black with the third Staffel being distinguished by the white circles painted on the fuselage. The three circles on the sides and top of the engine cowling were 500 mm (19.68 in) in diameter, the remaining four on the sides and above and below the rear fuselage were 400 mm (15.75 in) in diameter.

LEFT: An Ar 68 E piloted by the Gruppenadjutant of II./JG 334 makes its landing approach.

RIGHT: A Staffel of Ar 68 Fs neatly lined up for a photo call at Jesau in East Prussia during 1937. They belong to I./JG 131 which was formed from a nucleus provided by II./JG 132, its aircraft having black engine cowlings and fuselage top decking. These aircraft, from the second Staffel had white bands painted around the engine cowling and rear fuselage.

LEFT: Photographed at Jesau in East Prussia, this line-up of Ar 68 Fs are shown after delivery to I./JG 131. The aircraft have just received their black engine cowlings and upper fuselage decking, but the Staffel and individual markings have yet to be applied.

LEFT: Hptm. Hans-Günter von Kornatzki's Ar 68 E-1 after nosing over during taxying at Babenhausen-Hessen in 1937. At this time von Kornatzki, who was born on 22 June 1906 at Leignitz, was Gruppenadjutant of I./JG 334, his aircraft carrying a white chevron and bar marking. This marking was repeated on both sides of the fuselage and on the top of the upper wing centre section. After leading II./JG 52 for a short time, von Kornatzki was transferred to a training unit as an instructor in June 1940. During the summer of 1944 he formed the Sturmgruppe, II./JG 4, but was killed on 12 September.

BELOW: This Ar 68 E-1 was piloted by Fw. Franz Götz of 1./JG 334 based at Frankfurt-Rebstock. Götz was to serve with the Jagdwaffe throughout the Second World War, and awarded the Ritterkreuz on 4 September 1942. He served with III./JG 53 until the end of January 1945 when he became the last Kommodore of JG 26 "Schlageter".

LEFT: Ar 68 Es of 1./JG 334 seen here at Wiesbaden-Erbenheim. "White 6" is ready for action and "White 7" and "9" are undergoing routine engine checks. JG 334 was formed from a basis provided by JG 134, with these Ar 68s probably belonging to the former unit.

Arado Ar 68 E-1
Flown by Hptm. Hans-Günter von Kornatzki, Gruppenadjutant of I./JG 334, 1937. Unlike most of the other German fighter units of this later period, JG 334 does not appear to have had a "Traditional Colour" allocated to it. The white chevron and vertical bar marking was repeated on both sides of the fuselage as well as on top of the upper wing centre section.

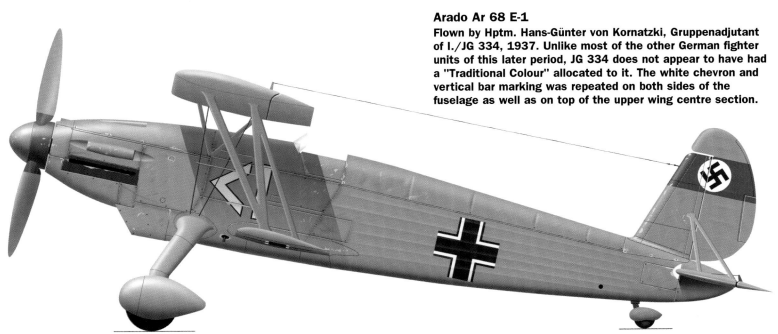

LEFT: A Kette of Ar 68 F-1s of 3./JG 131 at Jesau photographed in 1938. The cowlings, upper fuselage decking and rear fuselage band were painted black.

RIGHT: Hptm. Bernhard Woldenga (left), commander of I./JG 131, shows the controls of his Ar 68 to the deputy leader of the Nazi Party, Rudolf Hess. Hess was an accomplished pilot and a good friend of Willy Messerschmitt. Taken at Jesau in East Prussia during 1937, Woldenga's aircraft carries the white double chevron marking adopted for a Gruppenkommandeur.

LEFT: Oblt. Dietrich von Bothmer after receiving his promotion on 1 April 1937. At this time he was the most experienced member of 5./JG 134 "Horst Wessel", having returned from Spain where he claimed two victories. In the background can be seen a He 51 with the typical "Traditional" nose colour with the white band indicating the 2. Staffel and the horizontal bar indicating the II. Gruppe.

LEFT: Wearing dress uniform showing his new Oberleutnant rank patches, Dietrich von Bothmer, in the centre, being chauffeured to celebrate his promotion with his comrades. In the background is an Ar 68 F-1 of II./JG 134 "Horst Wessel". The aircraft "White 1" has a brown nose and upper fuselage decking which is also edged with a thin brown line. To von Bothmer's left is Lt. Hubertus von Holtey, Staffelkapitän of 5./JG 26 and Erg. St. JG 26.

RIGHT: On 2 July 1936 a new system of fighter markings was outlined in directive LA Nr.1290/36 geh LAQ II/Fl, designed to aid rapid air-to-air identification necessary during combat. Each Staffel was to have a white number from 1 to 12 edged in black painted in four positions: on each side of the fuselage, on top of the upper wing centre section and on the bottom of the fuselage between the wing roots. The size of the number was identical in all cases. These markings were introduced by September 1936 and are shown here on a He 51 of 1./JG 137 between June and July 1938.

RIGHT: Towards the end of 1937, with the establishment of Luftkreiskommando 7, I./JG 232 at Bernburg was redesignated I./JG 137. Led by Hptm. Hannes Gentzen, the 2. and 3. Staffel were to form the basis of I.(leicht Jagd)/ Lehrgeschwader 2 on 1 February 1938. JG 137 retained the green engine cowlings and upper fuselage decking of its predecessor, the white bands around the cowling and rear fuselage indicating that the He 51 B shown in this photo belonged to the newly reformed 2. Staffel.

LEFT AND BELOW: With the new Luftwaffe fighter marking system proposed on 2 July 1936, it was directed that a series of symbols was used in conjunction with the Staffel numbers. These were to identify the Staffel within the Gruppe and the Gruppe within the Geschwader. The 2. Staffel within a Gruppe was to have white bands painted around its engine cowlings and rear fuselage bands as is shown on these He 51 Bs of 2./JG 137 at Bernburg.

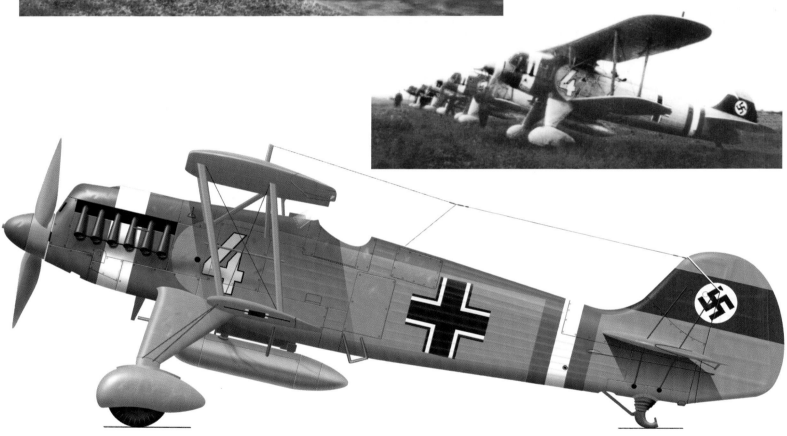

Heinkel He 51 B-1 of 2./JG 137

At Bernburg, early 1938, I./JG 137, which had been formed from I./JG 232 in October 1937, used the "Traditional Colour" green. The white band painted around the cowling was 300 mm (11.81 in) wide, those around the rear fuselage, 200 mm (7.87 in) each. These bands identified an aircraft of the second Staffel.

RIGHT: These highly polished He 51s belonged to 2./JG 137 based at Bernburg. This Geschwader had the cowlings and upper fuselage decking of its aircraft painted bright green, the white parts around the nose and rear fuselage indicating the second Staffel. The aircraft's individual numbers were painted white edged in black.

ABOVE: At the beginning of 1938 a group of Austrian fighter pilots from the Österreichische Jagdgruppe at Wien-Schwechat visited their German colleagues at Berlin-Döberitz. The first aircraft in this photo is a Fiat C.R. 30 B ("B" indicating twin seats), with a group of C.R. 32 B single-seaters behind.

LEFT: Generalmajor Wolff (centre) and Generaloberst Alexander Löhr salute Göring after German forces entered the Austrian town of Linz in March 1938. In Löhr, the former commander of the Austrian Air Force, Germany was to gain a very able leader who later led Luftflotte 4. He is seen here in his Austrian Air Force uniform.

RIGHT: After Austria was incorporated into Germany in March 1938, Hitler led a parade through the capital, Vienna. To Hitler's right in this picture is General Erhard Milch, Secretary of State in the new German Air Ministry while, to his right, is Generaloberst Fedor von Bock, commander of the troops entering Austria. Von Bock subsequently had several army commands, but was dismissed by Hitler and died in an air raid in 1945.

LEFT: Following the Austria Anschluss Hitler looked to further his expansionist aims by taking over the Sudetenland, a German-speaking area of Czechoslovakia. For this reason I./JG 131 was transferred, on 1 August 1938, to Liegnitz in Silesia, not far from the Czechoslovakian border. The unit was to stay in the area for three months by which time the Sudetenland had been successfully occupied. Here the Gruppenadjutant's Bf 109 D is readied for action by a group of mechanics from the unit.

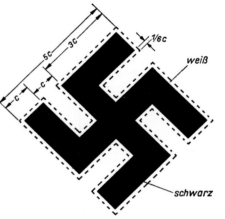

RIGHT: Standard proportions of Hakenkreuz taken from the official document.

weiß

schwarz

Abmessungen

Größe 5c	315	(400)	500	(630)	800	
c	63	80	100	126	160	
3c	189	240	300	378	480	
1/6c	10	13	17	21	27	

Auf Sichtschutzanstrich Farbton 70÷75 fällt schwarzes Innenteil des Hakenkreuzes fort.

ABOVE: Lt. Erwin Mann (left) and Oblt. Wilhelm Balthasar (Kapitän of 1./JG 131) standing in front of a Bf 109 D at Jesau during June or July 1938. Note the "Jesau Cross" insignia below the cockpit which was subsequently used by I./JG 130, I./JG 1 and III./JG 27 as the Gruppe was successively redesignated.

RIGHT: From 1936 the Luftwaffe fighter force was expanded rapidly by the so-called "Mutter und Tochter" ("Mother and Daughter") procedure in which parts of existing units were used to create new Gruppen. I./JG 131 was one of these, established at Jesau on 1 April 1937 from a nucleus provided by JG 132. This photo shows the Gruppenkommandeur, Hptm. Bernhard Woldenga, sitting in the cockpit of his Bf 109 D. Woldenga, who was awarded the Ritterkreuz on 5 July 1941, became Kommodore of JG 27 on 23 June 1941 and led the Geschwader until 7 June 1942 when he was appointed Fliegerführer Balkan.

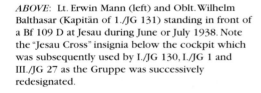

RIGHT: After being transferred to Liegnitz during the autumn of 1938, aircraft from I./JG 131 flew a number of operations over the Czechoslovakian border in support of Hitler's claim to the Sudetenland. A detachment of the unit was also transferred to Nieder-Ellguth near Oppeln where several officers were billeted in the castle owned by Gräfin (Countess) Siersdorf. Here the countess poses in front of the 2. Staffel Staffelkapitän's Bf 109 D coded "Red 1".

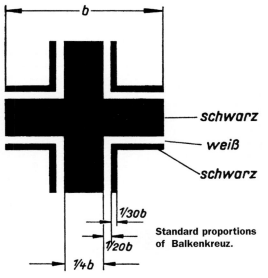

schwarz

weiß

schwarz

1/30 b

1/20 b

1/4 b

Standard proportions of Balkenkreuz.

BELOW AND COLOUR PROFILE: A Bf 109 C-1 of 1./JG 130 on an airfield at Gutenfeld in East Prussia during the summer of 1938.

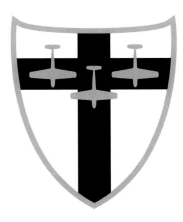

The "Jesau Kreuz"

Messerschmitt Bf 109 C-1 of 1./JG 130

At Gutenfeld in East Prussia, summer 1938, this aircraft carries the "Jesau Kreuz" badge, the insignia of the town where JG 130 was formed. This badge had been carried previously by aircraft of I./JG 131 and later by I./JG 1 and III./JG 27 which were successive redesignations of I./JG 131. Note that the marking of the Hakenkreuz has changed to a simple black shape edged in white.

LEFT: On 1 July 1938 a IV. Gruppe was added to JG 132 "Richthofen". Despite being in existence for a short time, IV./JG 132 supported German operations in the Sudeten crisis, the Gruppe being transferred first to Oschatz and then, on 5 October 1938, to Karlsbad. This photo Bf 109 Ds, from 10./JG 132, was taken shortly after arriving at their new base. On 1 November, the unit was redesignated I./JG 331 and on 1 May 1939 I./JG 77, by which time it had moved to Breslau.

ABOVE: At an early stage in its history, Jagdgeschwader Richthofen had a red script "R" painted on a white shield on both sides of the fuselage of its Bf 109s. This early Bf 109 E, "Yellow 10" probably of 3./JG 132 has black-green (70) and dark green (71) uppersurfaces with pale blue (65) beneath. 3./JG 132 was subsequently redesignated 3./JG 131 and 3./JG 2.

ABOVE AND COLOUR PROFILE: Bf 109 D-1 flown by Oberst Gerd von Massow, Geschwaderkommodore of JG 131 (later JG 2) "Richthofen", Döberitz, spring 1939. Massow's machine carried one of the alternative markings specified in the Luftwaffe directive issued on 14 December 1937, calling for two black horizontal bars, the forward one with a pointed tip. Von Massow led the Stab of the "Richthofen" Geschwader from 9 June 1936 to 31 March 1940.

Messerschmitt Bf 109 D-1
Flown by Oberst Gerd von Massow, Geschwader-kommodore of JG 131 (later JG 2) "Richthofen".

"Richthofen" badge

RIGHT: The arrival of IV./JG 132 at Karlsbad in the Sudetenland on 5 October 1938 was greeted by a large ceremony. These Bf 109 Ds of 11./JG 132 under Oblt. Erwin Neuerburg, carry red numbers on their fuselage sides and the famous script "R" insignia beneath the cockpit. The uppersurfaces of the aircraft were painted in black-green (70) and dark green (71) with the fuselage Balkenkreuz thinly outlined in white.

LEFT: A busy scene after 11./JG 132 arrived at Karlsbad in October 1938. It was normal at this time for the Hakenkreuz to be painted across both fin and rudder as can be seen from the tail of the Bf 109 D to the left of the picture. Note the large camouflaged pyramid shaped tent.

RIGHT: After occupying the Sudetenland in the autumn of 1938, the Luftwaffe took over a number of Czech aircraft. Perhaps most important of these was the Avia B 534 biplane which was used in some numbers by German advanced training units.

Neatly lined up in numerical order, this Staffel of Ar 68 F-1s was possibly flown by 1./JG 234 "Schlageter" based at Köln. This Geschwader, which was eventually to become JG 26, had orange engine cowlings and upper fuselage decking.

Arado Ar 68 F-1 of 1./JG 234 "Schlageter"
Depicted at Köln-Butzweilerhof, summer 1937. Like most Luftwaffe fighters of the period, JG 234's aircraft were given a primer coat of oil-based light grey, an undercoat of silver and a final coat of grey which had a green cast to it. The Gesschwader's "Traditional Colour" was bright orange.

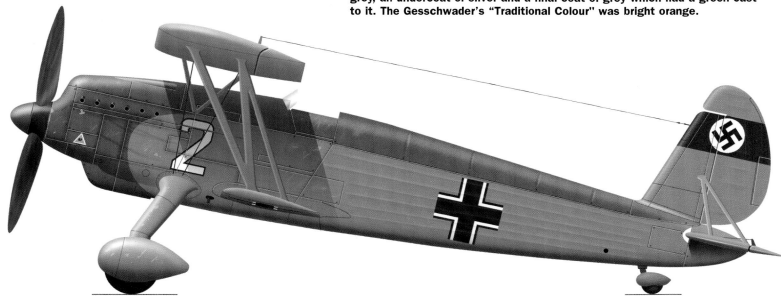

LEFT: Popularly known as the "Black Knight", Hptm. Eduard Ritter von Schleich was awarded the Pour le Mérite on 2 December 1917. He was to achieve 35 victories while serving first as commander of Jasta 32 and then the Bavarian Jagdgeschwader 4. After the First World War he became one of the earliest members of the Nazi Party and, for a time, a member of the SS. On 11 December 1938, when an Oberstleutnant, he became the first Kommodore of the newly established JG 132 "Schlageter" (not to be confused with JG 132 "Richthofen"). After the Second World War began he was appointed head of the Fighter Training School at Vienna, but retired before the German capitulation in May 1945.

BELOW: On 26 September 1938, the Luftwaffe still had 640 Arado 68 fighters equipping its Jagdgeschwader as compared with 171 Messerschmitt Bf 109s. By the following year this figure had been dramatically reversed, 747 Bf 109s being operational as against 28 Ar 68s. Note the Junkers W 34 in the background.

LEFT: Two pilots of JG 134 "Horst Wessel" honour one of their comrades killed during a training exercise during the spring of 1938. The flower and flag draped coffin is backed by two of the unit's new Bf 109 fighters. By this time the Messerschmitt fighter was gradually replacing the He 51s and Ar 68s with the Jagdwaffe. Hans Schmoller-Haldy who experienced the transition from the He 51 to the Bf 109 remembers that there were many severe accidents. The Bf 109 was not an easy aircraft to fly after the more placid biplanes.

BELOW: The first intake ("Lehrgang") of trainee Luftwaffe pilots at Jagdfliegerschule 1 at Werneuchen with their commander, Theo Osterkamp, in the centre. Osterkamp had been awarded the Pour le Mérite during the First World War when he scored 32 victories. To his left in this photo is Oblt. Gärtner. In the rank on the left, fourth from the left is the Jagdlehrer, Oblt. Hannes Trautloft and, at his right, Oblt. Walter Kienzle who was shot down and taken prisoner in Britain.

ABOVE: The black "F3C" marking on the fuselage sides of this Fw 44 was a racing number. Many German trainers were to take part in races during the 1930s.

BELOW: Three major versions of the He 72 *Kadett* two-seat primary trainer were built. The third variant, of which a line-up is seen here, was the He 72 C powered by the 140 hp Argus As 10 B in-line engine. These aircraft were delivered to the DVS at Berlin during April 1934. The type continued in use as a trainer until well after the outbreak of the war.

RIGHT: As has been described in the introduction, as the Luftwaffe increased in size, many new units were formed by the splitting of old ones. The birth of each new unit was usually accompanied by an impressive military ceremony held in the presence of high ranking officers. Here two Fw 44s are handed over to a newly created unit in 1937.

Focke-Wulf Fw 44 J-1
Possibly used as interim equipment by I./JG 135, April 1937. Because of the shortage of front-line fighters at this time, several of the Jagdgruppen used trainers such as the Fw 44 and He 72 as their interim equipment. These aircraft carried standard German civil registrations.

ABOVE: Before it was destroyed in a bombing raid later in the war, the Aviation Museum in Berlin possessed a large collection of German aircraft. This view of the main gallery gives an excellent idea of the scope of the collection.

RIGHT: The fourth prototype He 112, D-IZMY, was the first aircraft to be fitted with the production type elliptical wing somewhat similar to that of the British Spitfire. This photograph was taken at the Berlin air museum before it was destroyed in a bombing raid.

LEFT AND ABOVE A line-up of Ar 68 E-1 fighters of 3./JG 334 with white circles and white numbers. JG 334, unlike most other Luftwaffe fighter units of the perod, did not have a "Traditional Colour" to identify the unit's aircraft.

RIGHT: The guns of this Bf 109 B are being synchronised during a maintenance check. The aircraft carries the markings of the Kapitän of the fifth Staffel probably of Jagdgeschwader 132. The number "1" and horizontal bar were painted in red outlined in white.

LEFT: The Bf 109 D-1 differed from the Bf 109 C in reverting to the Jumo 210 Da engine, but it had a revised exhaust system with small stub-like outlets. Like the C-series, it carried an armament of four 7.9 mm MG 17 machine-guns, two above the engine and two in the wings.

LEFT AND BELOW: This Bf 109 D was belly landed by Uffz. Hugo Dahmer at Düsseldorf when he was with II./JG 234, (later II./JG 26), in early 1938. It carried a black double chevron and horizontal bar edged in white which indicated that it belonged to the Gruppenkommandeur of the second Gruppe, at that time Major Eduard von Schleich. The aircraft carries the Werknummer 447. It was not uncommon for pilots who had been used to fixed undercarriages to forget to lower the wheels of their Bf 109s when landing. Furthermore, the undercarriage of the Messerschmitt fighter was notoriously unreliable and often collapsed on landing.

LEFT: The same aircraft after being lifted back onto its undercarraige, indicating that there was nothing wrong with the hydraulic mechanism.

BELOW: A Staffel of Bf 109 D-1s with red numbers and red horizontal bars, both outlined in white. These aircraft carry a camouflage scheme of black-green (70) and dark green (71) on their uppersurfaces, the two colours divided by sharp jagged lines. In many photographs it is very difficult to see the difference between the two colours. The undersides of these aircraft were painted pale blue (65). Note that the white circle and red band has been omitted from the tails of these aircraft.

ABOVE: This Bf 109 D-1 of the second Gruppe of Jagdgeschwader 334 carries the single chevron which was specified for the second and third aircraft in the Gruppenstab. Note also the small number "White 1" in front of the chevron. After the war began a large variety of these staff symbols began to appear, many of them apparently conjured up at the will of the pilot and/or ground crews. Nevertheless, the symbols were nearly always painted black, outlined in white.

LEFT: A Bf 109 D-1 of 5./JG 334 comes in to land at Mannheim-Sandhofen with another Bf 109 from the same unit parked below. The number "3" and horizontal bar are painted red outlined in white as specified by the directive laid down by the Luftwaffe Generalstab on 14 December 1937, denoting the second Staffel within the Gruppe.

RIGHT: This time with a Junkers W 34 coming in to land, another photo of Bf 109 D-1 "Red 3" of 5./JG 334 taken at Mannheim-Sandhofen. The horizontal bar aft of the Balkenkreuz, also painted in red outlined in white, identifies the aircraft as belonging to the second Gruppe of the Geschwader.

ABOVE: Following the introduction of the marking scheme, it becomes very difficult for the historian to evaluate the identity of the unit to which a Bf 109 belongs unless a Geschwader or Gruppe emblem is visible. This Bf 109 D-1, which closely follows the directive, carries a red number "2" and horizontal bar, both outlined in red, indicating an aircraft of the 5. Staffel of JG 334 based at Mannheim in the late spring of 1938.

RIGHT: In spite of being appointed Oberbürgermeister (mayor) of the city of Wiesbaden, Dr. Erich Mix was still able to make frequent visits to I./JG 334 at Erbenheim. Promoted to Hauptmann in April 1938, he poses in front of one of the first Staffel's Bf 109s coded "White 10".

1937-1938

LEFT: By 1939 the B2 type Balkenkreuz with thick white outline and black edging, had replaced the old B1 style under the wings of the Luftwaffe's Bf 109s. These crosses, together with Swatiskas, have been detailed on page 324 of "JV 44 - The Galland Circus" published by Classic Publications.

BELOW: The Bf 109 D was to replace the earlier B and C models on the production line from 1938. This late D variant has the Bf 109 E exhaust stubs and fairing. The sub-type was still operational when the war began, but by early 1940, they had all been transferred to training units like these "Doras" seen here.

ABOVE: Lt. Herbert Huppertz (third from the left) photographed late in 1938 during his training on the Bf 109, probably with IV./JG 132. Entering the Luftwaffe in the autumn of 1937, Huppertz achieved his first victories with 3./JG 77 in 1940, this unit becoming 12./JG 51 on 24 August 1940.

LEFT: Some of the last production Bf 109 Ds were delivered to the Luftwaffe in the later style fighter camouflage with pale blue fuselage sides. These aircraft, from an unknown unit, but probably a training school, have their upper surfaces painted in either two greys (RLM colours 74 and 75) or perhaps in a mixture of dark green (71) and RLM grey (02). Many early C and D variants were ultimately transferred to training schools.

ABOVE: By the autumn of 1938 black-green and dark green camouflage with pale blue undersurfaces had begun to be introduced for Ar 68 fighters, replacing the pale grey finish with coloured sections used earlier. The camouflage was similar to that introduced for the Bf 109 during the summer of 1937.

ABOVE: It was by no means unusual for the wheel spats of the Ar 68 to be removed to ease maintenance. This aircraft has black-green and dark green uppersurfaces. Many early machines continued to see service but were gradually transferred to training schools.

ABOVE: Three pilots grouped around an Ar 68 E-1 of JG 134 at Neisse, Upper Silesia, September 1938. By this time, most Ar 68s were beginning to adopt dark green camouflaged uppersurfaces with pale blue beneath.

ABOVE: This Ar 68 is finished in the black-green (70) and dark green (71) camouflage with pale blue (65) undersurfaces which was introduced to replace the pale grey with coloured sections used earlier. The camouflage was similar to that introduced for the Bf 109 during the summer of 1937. Note the aircraft's "penguin" badge which bears a similarity to the emblem used later by III./ZG 26.

Arado Ar 68 E-1 of 9./JG 142 "Horst Wessel"
Based at Lippstadt, late spring 1939, III./JG 142 was formed from IV./JG 134 on 1 November 1938, the unit eventually becoming III./ZG 26 equipped with the Bf 110. This aircraft carries very similar markings to those proposed for the Bf 109 in 1937.

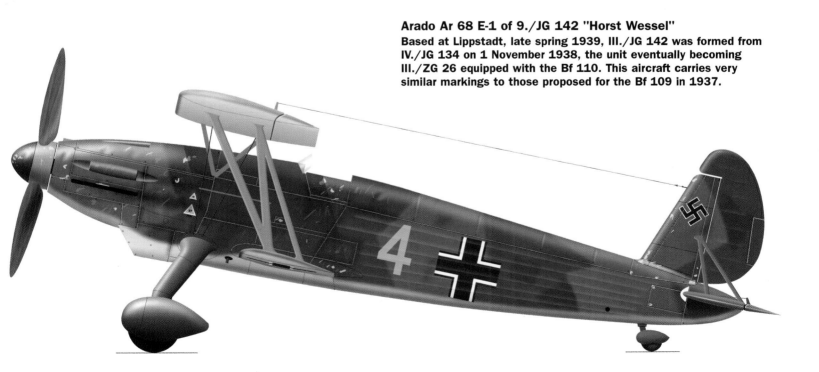

1937-1938

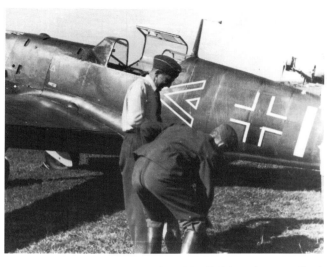

ABOVE: Late in 1938, I./JG 334 received its first Bf 109 Es. The Bf 109 progressively replaced the He 51, this photo, taken during the autumn of 1938, shows both types operational at Wiesbaden-Erbenheim.

BELOW: Just prior to the launching of Germany's first aircraft carrier, the Graf Zeppelin, on 18 December 1938, two Luftwaffe squadrons were formed to operate from the vessel: 4.(Stuka) and 6.(Jagd)/Trägergruppe 186. Both were formed at Kiel-Holtenau, the latter equipped initially with the twelve Bf 109 Bs shown here. In September 1939, a 5.(Jagd) Staffel was added, the two fighter squadrons then being redesignated II.(Jagd)/186 later in the month and placed under the command of Hptm. Heinrich Seeliger.

ABOVE: Max Ibel (seen here standing by his Bf 109 D-1), He later became the first Kommandeur of I./JG 135 when it was established in April 1937. He was later to form JG 27 on 1 October 1939, leading that Geschwader until 14 October 1940. The Bf 109 in the background has the double chevron of a Gruppenkommandeur painted in black outlined in white forward of the fuselage cross. Behind the national insignia is what appears to be a white bar but the significance of that marking at this time is unknown.

Heinkel He 112 B-0 of 12./JG 132
Based at Oschatz, September 1938, this type, which competed with the Bf 109, was only used operationally for a short time during the occupation of the Sudetenland. For this action, the aircraft carried similar camouflage to that introduced for the Bf 109. At this time, aircraft of the fourth Gruppe do not appear to have carried any special identification markings.

ABOVE: A He 112 B-0 "Yellow 4" of 12./JG 132

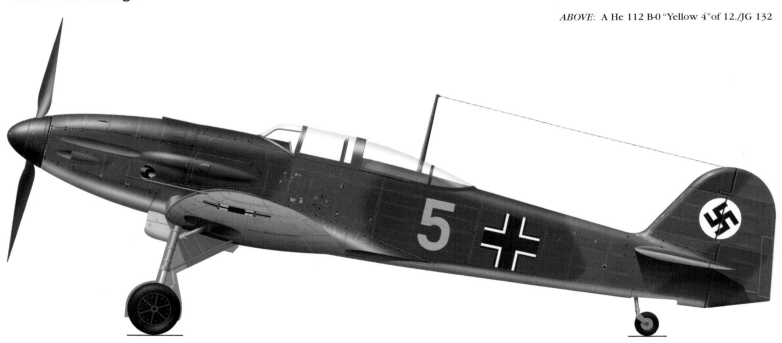

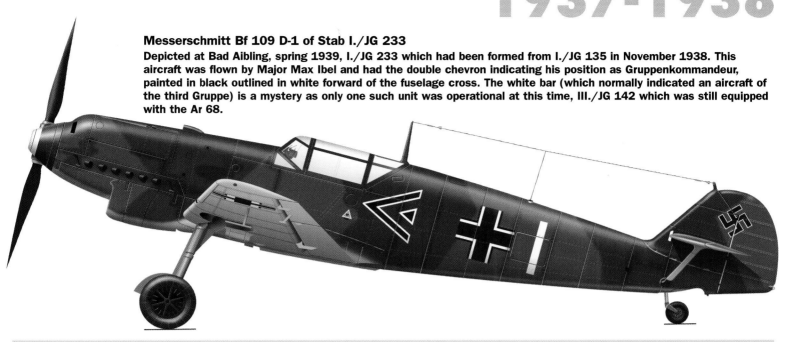

Messerschmitt Bf 109 D-1 of Stab I./JG 233
Depicted at Bad Aibling, spring 1939, I./JG 233 which had been formed from I./JG 135 in November 1938. This aircraft was flown by Major Max Ibel and had the double chevron indicating his position as Gruppenkommandeur, painted in black outlined in white forward of the fuselage cross. The white bar (which normally indicated an aircraft of the third Gruppe) is a mystery as only one such unit was operational at this time, III./JG 142 which was still equipped with the Ar 68.

"We took off with full armament for Austria..."

HANS SCHMOLLER-HALDY

"I was born in Mülhausen (actually in France) on 11 February 1911. Since the late 1920s I had a great interest in aviation. When I was 17-18, I had an opportunity to make a short passenger flight in a Fokker over the München area and was so impressed that I promised myself that I would become a pilot. This promise would change my whole life.

"In 1933, I was living in München when the National Socialists took power. One spoke much about the development of German aviation. One day, one of my directors (I worked at the Allianz-Versicherung company at the time) said: 'Schmoller-Haldy, you are young and strong, why don't you try to fly yourself?' At the end of 1933 the *Luftwaffe* did not exist officially, but had in fact been established secretly under the cover of sports associations. Nevertheless, their goal was clear, they would soon form the basis of a military air arm. So in 1934, I decided to volunteer here, in München.

"At that time we were a group of approximately ten men including two or three former soldiers of World War One and about six young men in their early twenties. We all six were accepted for military aviation, but something was soon clarified: 'If you want to become a pilot, you will be integrated into military aviation and will become a soldier!' To me it was not important, all I wanted to do was fly. I began training in the middle of 1934. The first step was to receive six months' military training, learning discipline and physical fitness. By Christmas 1934 I was a *Leutnant*. Then we underwent theoretical training before we saw our first aircraft. At last I was transferred to Salzwedel where I could begin flying, at first on the Heinkel *Kadett* and then the Focke-Wulf *Stieglitz*. Normal flying training lasted approximately 20 months with approximately 160 flying hours. After 30 hours initial training, I was transferred to Schleißheim in order to obtain my *B-Schein* (B-certificate) on single-engined aircraft. The following year I was trained in cross-country and aerobatic flying. I also began to train for the C-certificate on multi-engined aircraft, but did not gain this because I was selected for the *Jagdwaffe*. I was then transferred to a fighter unit at Bernburg, known as *"Jagdgruppe Bernburg"*. There I found in my roommate a comrade and excellent friend who would later become one of the greatest night fighter aces, Werner Streib.

"It was at this unit that I learned to be a fighter pilot. I was taught by such famous names as Eduard Neumann and Adolf Galland. At Bernburg we had frequent contact with our mother squadron, JG 132 based at Döberitz, because most of our teachers and officers came from this unit, such as Hans-Heinrich Brustellin and Werner Andres. We were equipped with the generally similar Ar 68 and He 51.

"In March 1937 one of the *Staffelkapitäne* of *Jagdgruppe Bernburg*, *Major* Max Ibel, received orders to create a new *Gruppe* to be known as I./JG 135. He chose me as Adjutant with *Hptm.* Hannes Trautloft (who had recently returned from Spain), as *Kapitän* of the 1. Staffel. Wolfgang Schellmann (who later became the second highest scoring German pilot in Spain) and *Oblt.* Meyer, an ex-reconnaissance pilot, led 2. and 3./JG 135 respectively. Soon after its formation, I./JG 135 was transferred to Bad Aibling, about 50 km south-east of München.

"During the evening of 11 March 1938, at about 19.00 hours, all *Staffelkapitäne* and pilots were called to Ibel's mess who told us that we were to be placed on instant alert. Our mechanics had to prepare every available aircraft and the pilots could not leave the airfield. Next day, we were up at 07.00 hours and were ready for action two hours later. We joked in front of the mess with our little packages of personal belongings, wondering what was going on. Then we took off with full armament for Austria, heading for Linz. At last we understood. Germany was going to attempt the annexation (or was it the invasion?) of Austria and we might be called upon to fight with certain factions of the Austrian Air Force. Fortunately all went peacefully and after a short stay at Linz, our *Gruppe* was installed on the airfield of Aspern near Vienna where we had nothing to do.

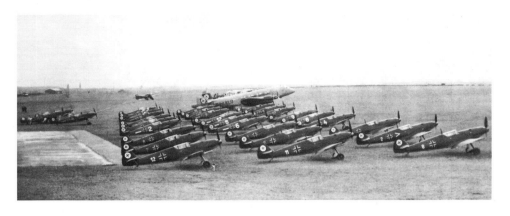

LEFT: Although the marking system for Bf 109s had been laid down in the directive of 14 December 1937, this photo of a group of aircraft of JG 133 at Wiesbaden-Erbenheim, taken in the late spring of 1939, shows that it was not always followed. The four aircraft in the foreground, belonging to the first *Staffel*, had small white numbers positioned aft of the fuselage Balkenkreuz. A similar scheme was followed by the aircraft of the second and third *Staffeln* except that the colour of the number was red and yellow respectively. Behind these Bf 109 B-2s can be seen a number of aircraft from the second *Gruppe* which closely followed the December 1937 directive, with the numbers painted forward of the cross and the *Gruppe* symbols aft. In the background can be seen a Ju 90 communications aircraft, D-AALU, and a Ju 87 A.

"Our Staffeln only numbered three or four pilots each..."

GERHARD SCHÖPFEL

In December 1941, Gerhard Schöpfel was appointed Adolf Galland's successor as *Kommodore* of JG 26. He later served as a fighter operations officer in southern Italy, as *Jafü Norwegen, Jafü Ungarn* and he also led JG 4 and JG 6 for periods as their *Kommodore*. From a total of 700 missions, he has been accredited with 40 victories, all scored in the West, the majority of which were RAF fighters. He was awarded the *Ritterkreuz* following his twentieth victory. Here, he recalls the early days of his service with the *Luftwaffe*:

"In 1932, the year I decided to enlist, the German Army only had an effective strength of 100,000 men. It was thus very hard to find a place in the Army's ranks and many volunteers went to the *Landespolizei*. So it was that in 1934, I went to a police officer school at Potsdam. It was there that I heard that the *Luftwaffe* was in the process of reconstruction and that opportunities existed for volunteers in this arm of the services. At that time, neither German civil or military aviation was particularly advanced in terms of technical development and strength. For my part, I had never been in the air, but I had nevertheless - like many young men of the time - been attracted by aviation, so I quickly decided to volunteer for the fledgling *Luftwaffe*. Despite suffering from vertigo since my boyhood, I immediately opted to become a pilot, and by doing so, avoided the other arms of the service such as the *Flak*, Intelligence or Signals (the *Luftnachrichttruppe*). Generally speaking, younger officers volunteered for the *Luftwaffe* where there were certain age limitations, whilst others preferred the infantry or the navy.

"I undertook various training courses and following these, I became firstly an observer and radioman before finally being posted to a fighter squadron at Brandenburg without actually attending a fighter school. The structure of the *Jagdwaffe* at this stage was developing so quickly that very often one received final training at one's assigned unit. Specific fighter training units would only be formed several years later and trainee pilots would be instructed by experienced fighter pilots. But this was not the case in 1936-37.

"At that time, there was only one *Jagdgruppe* in Germany and every six months or so it was split or redesignated to accommodate the arrival of new pilots. At first, I was assigned to I./JG 132, the *"Richthofen Geschwader"* based at Berlin-Döberitz., but it was not long before all this was changed. The unit was split again and was redesignated under a new number and a new base; this time I was with I./JG 135 at Bad Aibling. Our *Kommandeur* at the time was the well-known, Max Ibel and we had in our unit, men such as Hannes Trautloft (*Staffelkapitän* of 1. *Staffel*), Wolfgang Schellmann (*Staffelkapitän* of 2. *Staffel*) and Hans-Heinrich Brustellin (*Staffelkapitän* of 3. *Staffel*) as well as Eduard Neumann and Dietrich Hrabak - all pilots who would go on to become leading *Luftwaffe* aces or highly regarded wartime formation commanders.

"In 1937, our *Gruppe* was the only one to be based in the area of *Luftkreis* 5 and it was for this reason that we were involved in the advance into Austria. Our three component *Staffeln* were based on different airfields there by March 1938. Whilst in Austria, the *Gruppe* raised one *Staffel* almost exclusively comprised of Austrian pilots. At this time, our pilots were continually drawn upon to reinforce the units of the *Legion Condor* serving in Spain. Such was the demand, that often our *Staffeln* numbered only three or four pilots each, the rest being transferred to Spain. If any unit suffered a crash or accident, it had to wait a long time for a replacement aircraft.

"I was then posted to JG 26 based in the West. Our *Geschwaderstab* and I./JG 26 were based at Köln/Ostheim and the other *Gruppe*, II./JG 26 was based at Düsseldorf, the *Geschwader's* "home town". In Düsseldorf, these was a regional *Gauleiter* named Florian who had flown as a fighter pilot with the Richthofen squadron during the First World War and he very much wanted to link the name of his city with one of the newly formed *Jagdgeschwadern*. In fact, in 1938, the High Command wanted to bestow an "honour title" to all the *Geschwadern*, such names usually being selected from amongst the most well known fliers from the First World War. For example, JG 132 became known as the *"Richthofen Geschwader"*, *Stukageschwader 2* became the *"Immelmann Geschwader"* and KG 27 was named after *"Boelcke."*

"The *Gauleiter* obtained instruction from Hitler that we should be named after a German officer, Albert Leo Schlageter, who had been instrumental in the resistance against the French occupation of Düsseldorf. Schlageter was finally shot in 1937.

"At JG 26 *"Schlageter"*, I was already considered an "old" experienced pilot and when the third *Gruppe* was later formed at Werl in September 1939, I was appointed the *Staffelkapitän* of its 9. *Staffel*."

Markings of aircraft belonging to light fighter units
Translation of Directive Fl.In.3 Nr 730/37 II issued by the Luftwaffe Generalstab on 14 December 1937

All previous orders regarding the markings of light fighter units' aircraft are cancelled.

The following markings are introduced with immediate effect.

I. Application of markings

National insignia (*Balkenkreuz and Hakenkreuz*) as before.

Markings will be applied on both sides of the fuselage sides only.

In order to create a uniform image, location and dimensions as shown on attached diagrams are to be strictly observed.

II. Form and schematic of unit markings

Markings of the *Staffel* aircraft.

a) *Staffel* aircraft (including reserve aircraft) to carry the Arabic numerals from 1 to 12, i.e.

    1., 4. and 7. Staffel in white without border

    2., 5. and 8. Staffel in red with white border

    3., 6, and 9. Staffel in yellow (loam yellow - sic) with black border

b) *Gruppe* and *Gruppe* Staff symbols

    I. *Gruppe* of the *Geschwader* carries no symbol

    II. *Gruppe*, a horizontal bar behind the *Balkenkreuz* an the respective *Staffel* colour and border.

    III. *Gruppe*, a vertical bar, also in the *Staffel* colour and border.

Gruppen aircraft carry a chevron with a triangular section in black with white border in place of the numeral. The *Gruppen* symbol (as above) is also black with white border.

    The two wingmen of the *Gruppen* staff are to be marked similarly to the *Gruppen* leader's aircraft, however, without the black triangle.

c) *Geschwader* emblem and markings of the three *Geschwader* Staff aircraft

The *Geschwader* leader's aircraft is to carry an arrow, its shaft extending as far as the horizontal stabiliser. Colour is to be black with white border.

    The two wingmen are to carry a pointed bar only, without the arrowhead.

    For *Geschwader* identification, a space of 250 x 300 mm (9.8 x 11.8 inch) is reserved (see illustration). The individual *Geschwader* emblem is to be applied in this space.

    All *Geschwader Kommodores* and *Kommandeure* of independant *Gruppen* are to submit proposals for such symbols before 1 February 1938. Emblems are only to be applied after authorisation from the R.d.L and Ob.d.L.[1]. The dimensions of 250 x 300 mm are to be strictly adhered to.

    This order applies only to Bf 109 fighter aircraft. Remarking of He 51 and Ar 68 aircraft is not necessary, since these types will be retired on delivery of the Bf 109. A separate order for heavy fighters will be published at a later date.

    Genst.d.L., 14.12.37,
Fl.In.3 Nr.730/37 II.

---

1 *Reichsminister der Luftfahrt (Minister of Aviation) and Oberbehelfhaber der Luftwaffe (Commander in Chief of the Air Force)*

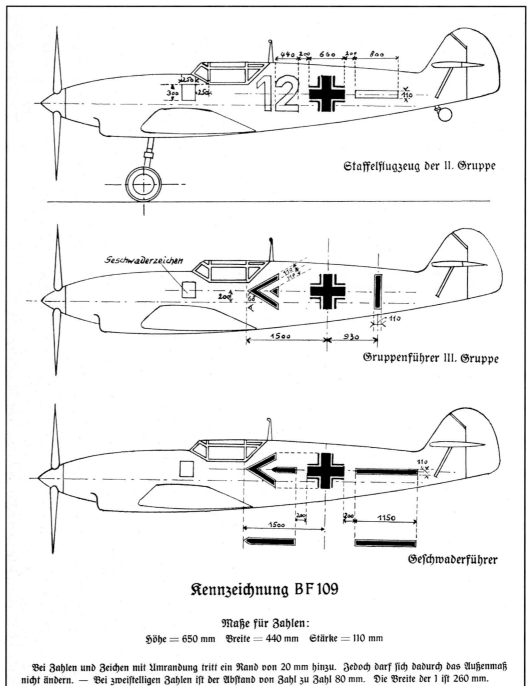

Staffelflugzeug der II. Gruppe

Geschwaderzeichen

Gruppenführer III. Gruppe

Geschwaderführer

Kennzeichnung BF 109

Maße für Zahlen:

Höhe = 650 mm   Breite = 440 mm   Stärke = 110 mm

Bei Zahlen und Zeichen mit Umrandung tritt ein Rand von 20 mm hinzu. Jedoch darf sich dadurch das Außenmaß nicht ändern. — Bei zweistelligen Zahlen ist der Abstand von Zahl zu Zahl 80 mm. Die Breite der 1 ist 260 mm.

DIMENSIONS FOR NUMERALS:

Height = 650 mm

Width = 440 mm

Thickness = 110 mm.

For numerals with border, a 20 mm edge is to be added, external measurements remain unchanged. for two digits, the distance between numerals is 80 mm, the width of the "1" is 260 mm.

Messerschmitt Bf 109 B-2 of 6./JG 133
At Wiesbaden-Erbenheim, winter 1938-39, JG 133 was formed from JG 334 on 1 November 1938, this Bf 109 having black-green (70) uppersurfaces with pale blue (65) beneath. The aircraft's number and second Gruppe bar were painted bright yellow (04) with black edging.

ABOVE: This line-up of Bf 109 Bs probably of II./JG 133, display some interesting variations in markings. The second aircraft has the individual number "12" in yellow edged in black with the horizontal bar of the second Gruppe in a similar colour. This would identify an aircraft of 6./JG 133. The third aircraft carries a black single chevron edged in white, indicating an aircraft belonging to the Gruppe Adjutant, and the fourth machine carries a white number 5, identifying it as belonging to the fourth Staffel. The tail of the Bf 109 nearest the camera carries the W.Nr.436 on the fin.

LEFT: Oblt. Hannes Trautloft (left) and Major Max Ibel of JG 135 admiring the performance of the Bf 109 D at Bad Aibling in 1938.